Questions You Shouldn't Ask About the Church

Stephen M. Miller
Editor

Cheri W. Lindsley
Editorial Assistant

Cover Photo: Dave Anderson

The following versions of Scripture have been used by permission:

All Bible quotations taken from *The Holy Bible, New International Version* (NIV) unless otherwise noted. Copyright © 1978 by the New York International Bible Society.

The Living Bible (TLB), © 1971 by Tyndale House Publishers, Wheaton, Ill.

The *New Testament in Modern English* (Phillips), Revised Edition © J. B. Phillips, 1958, 1960, 1972. By permission of the Macmillan Publishing Co.

The *New American Standard Bible* (NASB), © The Lockman Foundation, 1960, 1962, 1963, 1968, 1971, 1972, 1973, 1975, 1977.

The *Good News Bible, Today's English Version* (TEV)—New Testament © American Bible Society, 1966, 1971, 1976.

The *Revised Standard Version of the Bible* (RSV), copyrighted 1946, 1952, © 1971, 1973.

The King James Version (KJV).

ISBN: 083-410-9301

Printed in the United States of America

Questions You Shouldn't Ask About the Church

Published for the ALDERSGATE ASSOCIATES
By Beacon Hill Press of Kansas City
Kansas City, Missouri

Other Dialog Series Books

For a description of all available Dialog Series books, including some that may not be listed here, contact your publishing house and ask for the free Dialog Series brochure.

Contents

Chapter 1

Is Our Church Stuck in the Mud?

by Dean Merrill and Marshall Shelley

Background Scripture: Matthew 12:6; Ephesians 4:1-16

*D*AVID ELTON TRUEBLOOD *was born, as he likes to say, "in the last month of the last century" (December 1900). That tells you something about his mind; it is always taking note of things others miss. He has a ready explanation for why he retired from teaching philosophy at Earlham College promptly at age 65: "So people wouldn't ask me why I didn't."*

From 60 years of teaching, writing, and preaching (he was recorded as a Quaker minister when Warren G. Harding was president, and served as chaplain at Stanford for a decade), in this interview he talks about the well-being of the contemporary church.

Pastors and lay leaders, like everyone else, are prone to quiz themselves: "How am I doing? How is my church doing?" Are these good questions to ponder? Can they be asked too often?

Yes, there is a danger in asking them too much, because we are likely to become too aware of our own personal success.

7

That is bad. The questions encourage us to become too self-centered.

But it is good to ask, "Are we increasing Christ's kingdom? Are we in any sense doing what He intended when He invented the Church?"

I use the word *invented* deliberately, since there was no Church before Christ. An amazing invention it was, something far more revolutionary than we normally suppose.

I think we are too easily satisfied with conventional success. We fall back into an Old Testament mind-set, in which we look mostly at how many people come to the Temple for the ritual. That was what counted most under the old covenant. Meanwhile, we forget Jesus' words in Matthew 12:6—"I tell you, something greater than the temple is here" (RSV).

Cheap Christianity can usually pull a pretty good attendance on Sunday morning. It is cheap whenever the people think of themselves as spectators at a performance. I'm always shocked when I hear Christians talk about being *"in the audience."* Audiences are fine at the opera or the symphony concert, but worship is another matter.

In Christ's clearest call to commitment, He didn't say, "Come join the audience." He said, "Take my yoke upon you, and learn of me" (Matthew 11:29, KJV). The yoke refers to the operation of a team. Early Christians called each other "yoke-fellow" (Philippians 4:3, KJV) in order to signify a practicing, operating Christian, one engaged on a team effort.

So when leaders ask how the general operation is going, they must not be too easily satisfied with numbers. You can always get a crowd if you demand very little and put on a show. The promoters of the rock festival near San Bernardino last Labor Day got 200,000 to come and listen to loud music non-stop day and night. But if high demands are raised, the situation is far different.

How would you define a healthy fellowship?

A healthy fellowship is a redemptive fellowship. It is penetrating the world not for its own aggrandizement but to change the world. Almost all of Christ's metaphors for the Church are

8

penetrators—salt to penetrate the food and keep it from decay, light to penetrate the darkness, leaven to penetrate the lump. The emphasis is never on the instrument but on the function. So a successful church is one that is changing the world, chiefly through the action of its members.

The members, by the way, are wonderfully placed. Some of them are in offices, some in banks, some in factories, many in homes, many in schools. The way we make the church grow is by making the members more effective in penetration.

The most exciting thing I know here in Richmond is a soup-and-salad luncheon every Thursday for men, all of whom are ministers in common life. Physicians, lawyers, factory workers, businessmen of all kinds, and even a few pastors meet at the library of the First Friends Meetinghouse exactly at noon. We close exactly at 1:00—not 1:01—because these are people with responsibilities to keep. We begin with prayer, led by someone in the group, not an imported professional. We have our simple lunch, prepared by the women of the church, and leave our $2.00 on the table. At 12:20 we introduce new people, and then one of the group speaks for 16 minutes, sharing something that has strengthened his life in the ministry. Last come questions and answers, with great freedom, and a closing prayer. We average more than the Rotary Club in town—65 men on a normal Thursday.

Are these all from the Friends church?

Oh, no—that would destroy the idea. The mayor, who is Roman Catholic, is nearly always there. They come from all over—the only thing we have in common is that we are all ministers in daily life. We have no officers, no structure, no budget, no minutes, no reporting—that's what wears people out. We simply want to help each other penetrate the world.

Groups like this are going now in Muncie, Ind., and Wichita, Kans., and I hope it spreads farther.

I suppose I'm acting as sort of a pastor to the local group, in that I take more responsibility. But I am simply a coach. The pastor as coach is miles away from the idea of pastor as priest. The pastor as coach is not satisfied with good ritual and good buildings; he is satisfied only when people are being recruited into the ministry of daily life.

How do you know whether your friends on Thursday are actually penetrating the world or just showing up for lunch?

Well, here's one measure: How many of them are visiting in the jail? We got a fellow out of jail two weeks ago who apparently had been arrested unjustly. I went to the prosecuting attorney here in Richmond and persuaded him to drop charges. The point is, I could go to bat for the man because of my life here. I was listened to, while he never would have been.

At lunch the next Thursday, I told what had happened and gave the man's name and address. One of the group said, "I'll go and see him." He found him in a poor little shack—the man, his wife, and child with almost no food. So my friend got the members of his church to stock their pantry.

This is no big thing, but it's concrete. At other times, those in our group who sell cars have arranged decent transportation for people who otherwise couldn't afford it.

This kind of penetration is not so easily put into an annual report. Attendance and money are easy to write up for the annual business meeting, but you can never have a full report of the ministry of penetration. You will, however, see examples of it. What I most want people to realize is that this is expected, this is what the church requires.

Church is more than an hour a week. That is what I was trying to say when I wrote *Your Other Vocation*—that the Christian always has a two-pronged life. He or she must be a competent journalist or lawyer or industrialist—and must also be in the ministry of Christ in the world.

In your autobiography you wrote, "An untrained ministry is potentially harmful." So there's more to being a healthy church than just mobilization?

Absolutely. Jesus said not only "Take my yoke upon you" but also "Learn of me." The church must become a seminary if it is going to have a universal ministry. The pastor is the ideal person to be the dean of the seminary, drawing out the ministry of others, equipping, enabling. Those potent words of Christ, "Learn of me," will change our whole focus on ministry.

What if the pastor says, "I may be the dean, but I have no faculty. I am alone"?

He has to develop his faculty by training some of the members to train others. He must not fail to make a start.

What should be the curriculum of this "seminary"?

The first task is to deepen the spiritual lives of the people. So many today live so superficially. We can awaken and enrich them through the classics of Christian devotion—a rich body of material that is mostly unknown. If I were a pastor, I'd spend nearly all of my time teaching, and I would start right off with a class on these 10 books:

> Augustine's *Confessions*
>
> *The Little Flowers of St. Francis*
>
> *The Imitation of Christ,* by Thomas à Kempis
>
> The *Devotions* of John Donne
>
> Pascal's *Pensées*
>
> *The Journal of John Woolman*
>
> *A Serious Call to a Devout and Holy Life,* by William Law
>
> *Doctor Johnson's Prayers*
>
> *The Christian's Secret of a Happy Life,* by Hannah Whitall Smith
>
> Thomas Kelly's *Testament of Devotion*

All of these are in paperback and in good modern-English editions. Any ordinary person can grow tremendously through this type of material.

Most people don't know how to pray, for example. What better way to teach them than through Samuel Johnson's prayers? At the end of his life, in desperate sickness, he asked his physician how many more days he would live. The doctor estimated two, barring a miracle. "Very well," he replied. "Stop all medication, though the pain be terrible, for I would meet my

11

Maker with a clear mind." He then wrote this prayer, the last thing he penned:

> Almighty and most merciful Father, I am now, as to human eyes it seems, about to commemorate, for the last time, the death of Thy Son Jesus Christ our Savior and our Redeemer. Grant, O Lord, that my whole hope and confidence may be in His merits and His mercy; enforce and accept my imperfect repentance; make this commemoration available to the conformation of my faith, the establishment of my hope, and the enlargement of my charity; and make the death of Thy Son Jesus Christ effectual to my redemption. Have mercy upon me, and pardon the multitude of my offences. Bless my friends; have mercy upon all men. Support me, by the grace of Thy Holy Spirit, in the days of weakness, and at the hour of death; and receive me, at my death, to everlasting happiness, for the sake of Jesus Christ. Amen.

That teaches not only the devotional life; it teaches theology. If we don't raise the sights of people with this kind of training, they will pray in strings of clichés. We must soak them with great models.

There are other parts of the curriculum for a healthy church, of course—the Old and New Testaments, theology, the history of Christian thought, Socratic logic, Christian ethics. I have dwelt upon the devotional classics only because they are so often ignored.

You spend a lot of time with laypeople; you talk with many of them when their pastors are not in the room. Do they care about these things? Are they concerned about the health of their churches?

I hear them saying they are dissatisfied because they are not getting the kind of education that would develop them. They assume these great courses are going on in the theological seminaries, and they think their minds are equally as good as the students there, so they want to know why they're being cheated. They are tired of the tough questions being avoided.

When I talk with these people, I don't call them laymen. A layman is a second-class citizen. I am a layman in regard to law because I have not passed the bar; thus, I am not allowed to practice law. There is no place in the Church of Jesus Christ for those who cannot practice. I say to people, "You are not a layman. You are a minister of common life."

It almost sounds like a staff title.

I was so pleased with one signboard I saw outside a church in South Carolina. It read:

MINISTERS: ALL THE MEMBERS
EQUIPPER: REV. JOHN SMITH

The true ministers were the folk in the pews.

I would be willing to ordain people to the ministry of journalism, or banking, or photography—why not? What an opportunity they have. They meet people I will never meet. Think of the chances a loan officer has to minister: He can keep young people from ruining their lives by overborrowing.

The worst story I know—and I am told it is a true story—is about the preacher who came to Laymen's Sunday, the first Sunday of October, and preached on the lay ministry. (That was his first mistake; he should have had one of the members do it.) He was persuasive, however, because at the end, when he said, "Will any men who are willing to dedicate themselves to the lay ministry please come forward?" a hundred men responded. And someone who was right close to the pastor heard him mutter softly, "O God, how can I use a hundred ushers?"

He entirely missed the point of his own sermon.

I do not mean to diminish the pastorate—I make it vastly larger. I call pastors to engage not in Operation Addition but in Operation Multiplication. This is the point of Ephesians 4. For the pastor to think he is the only minister is to minimize the task.

Having observed the North American church for 60 years, do you think it is getting healthier or sicker?

Both. I can name places where the universal ministry is being developed, but they are few. I do, however, see some real gains. First, we have at last come to a widespread recognition that the church and the building are two different things. People do understand that the true church is not the structure on Jackson Avenue; it is where one person is teaching philosophy and another is cobbling shoes and another is teaching kindergarten. In this we are getting back to the New Testament. If you had gone to ancient Corinth and asked where the Christian church was, nobody would have sent you to the corner of Eighth and Main. They would have sent you to where Paul and his friends were making mobile homes—tents, that is. He himself explained this on Mars Hill when he said, "The God who made the world . . . does not live in shrines made by man" (Acts 17:24, RSV).

You said a few years back that faith has three essential aspects: the inner life of devotion, the outer life of service, and the intellectual life of rationality. How is the third area doing?

Well, it needs lifting, too; all three legs of the stool are essential. We must teach people to *pray,* to *serve,* and to *think.*

How do you teach people to think?

Chiefly by dialogue. That's what Plato said. One person's thinking stirs another person's thinking.

Tonight I have a group of young pastors and their wives coming here to talk. (Now that I'm liberated, I can use my time for things like this without asking a committee.) We're going to deal with hard intellectual problems, so they can return to their churches and do the same.

What will you talk about?

We're going to talk about how to be fair to other religions without compromising Christ's claim to be the only Way. This is the hardest intellectual problem many of them face. So I must help them.

Why? Because the Christian must outthink the world.

Almost 40 years ago you wrote, "The terrible danger of our time consists in the fact that ours is a *cutflower civilization."* Are the flowers dead yet?

Almost. One of the saddest things in my life is that my

prediction has come true. Look at the decay of so many people through drug abuse. Millions have ruined their lives this way, chiefly because they were so empty. They grasped for significance and elation, only to destroy themselves.

The loss of emphasis on chastity is a terrible loss. I go to many universities, and in almost none of them is a good word ever said about chastity. Promiscuity is assumed, even condoned, and in some cases encouraged. The flowers have been cut from their sustaining roots.

Thus it is more important than ever for the Church to be healthy. The Church is what I believe in. I know it is often poor and dull, but it's the best thing we've got, and I thank God for it. So when I drive through the country and see a little meetinghouse, I always take off my hat. They may have had some awfully poor preaching there, but when I think of the sacrifice, the dedication represented in that little place, I'm grateful.

However sick the Church is, our land would be an awfully lot sicker without it. It's our best hope. That's why I want to encourage it and make it dissatisfied with low standards.

If we could see the Church as a society of ministers in the world, we would approach the radical change Christ sought to initiate. If that were generally accepted, the change would not be small. It would be enormous. Christ did not seek to build a little thing. The chief way you and I are disloyal to Him is when we make small what He intended to make large.

Chapter 2

What's So Special About the Church?

by Eugene L. Stowe

Background Scripture: Numbers 9:15-21, 23; Acts 2:4, 42-47

WHERE IS YOUR CHURCH?"

"It's at the corner of 12th and Main."

Does that sound familiar? Most of us have responded to such a question with a similar answer. And it's partially true. On any given Sunday that's where you would find the congregation. But suppose next Saturday night a fire should break out in the furnace room of that building and destroy everything. Where would the church be then?

When people came to Sunday School or worship service the next morning, you would have to tell them that services are going to be held in the auditorium of the high school at 30th and State. That's where the church would be located until a new structure could be built. This illustrates a very important truth: THE CHURCH IS A BODY, NOT A BUILDING.

This is something very special about the church. Actually, the word "church" is a New Testament term. It is translated from the Greek word *ecclesia* which literally means "the called out ones." This makes it clear that churches are people—not places.

The association between buildings and worship began thousands of years before Christ created the concept of the Church. Two structures were vitally important in the religious life of God's people.

The Tabernacle

As children, many of us studied about this very interesting worship center. You may have made a model of it in Sunday School or Vacation Bible School. Chapters 25; 26; and 27 of the Book of Exodus describe it in detail. It is important to note that the Tabernacle was God's idea. He commanded Moses, "Let them make me a sanctuary; that I may dwell among them" (Exodus 25:8, KJV).

Before that message to Moses, Jehovah had been with His people ever since He created Adam and Eve in the Garden of Eden. After the Fall He spoke to Noah and gave him instructions about how to build the ark. After the Flood "the Lord came down to see the city and the tower" (Genesis 11:5, KJV). He communicated directly with Abraham and the other patriarchs, and they built altars where they could make sacrifices to Him. But now, for the first time, God associated His presence with a place.

The Tabernacle teaches us two very important spiritual truths:

1. *This portable sanctuary is God's guarantee that He will be with His people wherever they go.* The children of Israel were on the move. The Tabernacle was completely mobile. It was a tent which could be taken down and put up each time God's people moved. Numbers 9:15-21 and 23 speaks of His presence as the Cloud which overshadowed Israel:

> On the day the Tabernacle was raised, the Cloud covered it; and that evening the Cloud changed to the appearance of fire, and stayed that way throughout the

17

night. It was always so—the daytime Cloud changing to the appearance of fire at night. When the Cloud lifted, the people of Israel moved on to wherever it stopped, and camped there. In this way they journeyed at the command of the Lord and stopped where he told them to, then remained there as long as the Cloud stayed. If it stayed a long time, then they stayed a long time. But if it stayed only a few days, then they remained only a few days; for so the Lord had instructed them. Sometimes the fire-cloud stayed only during the night and moved on the next morning. But day or night, when it moved, the people broke camp and followed. ... So it was that they camped or traveled at the commandment of the Lord; and whatever the Lord told Moses they should do, they did *(TLB)*.

Later on God would confirm His continual presence to Joshua, the new leader of His people, in these words: "As I was with Moses, so I will be with thee: I will not fail thee, nor forsake thee" (Joshua 1:5, KJV).

Centuries later Paul identified the Church as a Body, not a building—"Now you are the body of Christ, and each one of you is a part of it" (1 Corinthians 12:27). The promise of God's perpetual presence was just as valid then as it was when He traveled with the Tabernacle. Jesus assured His disciples, "And surely I will be with you always, to the very end of the age" (Matthew 28:20). That means us too!

2. *The Tabernacle is also symbolic of God's personal direction of His Body, the Church.* He guided Israel through the wilderness by the Cloud which always hovered over the Tabernacle. When His people followed this mobile temple, they made progress toward the Promised Land. Years later God would inspire the prophet Isaiah to write: "And if you leave God's paths and go astray, you will hear a Voice behind you say, 'No, this is the way; walk here'" (Isaiah 30:21, TLB).

The Church (Christ's Body) was born on the Day of Pentecost when the Holy Spirit was poured out on 120 believers gathered in the Upper Room. One of the members of the Body was a layman named Philip. The Spirit became his personal

Guide. In Acts chapter 8 we see Philip following the leadership of the Spirit down the road from Jerusalem through the Gaza Desert. There he encountered the treasurer of Ethiopia riding home in his chariot. Verse 29 tells us that "the Holy Spirit said to Philip, 'Go over and walk along beside the chariot'" (TLB). He then explained the plan of salvation to the Ethiopian and helped him accept Christ as his personal Savior.

This same guidance is the legacy of the Church today. Christians enjoy the high privilege of having their lives directed by the Holy Spirit. Every day is an adventure as they follow His leadership and cooperate with His will. This makes life worth living!

The Temple

This is the second "church" building mentioned in the Old Testament. It was a far cry from the Tent-Tabernacle. God chose its location and its builder:

> I have never before, since bringing my people from the land of Egypt, chosen a city anywhere ... as the location of my Temple where my name will be glorified; ... But now I have chosen Jerusalem as that city *(2 Chronicles 6:5-6, TLB).*

King David had planned to build this magnificent Temple in Jerusalem. But God told him that hands stained with the blood of many battles could not construct this house of peace. Therefore, his son Solomon undertook this task.

The building is described in 2 Chronicles chapters 2—4. It was not very large—just 90 feet long, 30 feet wide, and 45 feet high. A work force of 150,000 men with 3,600 foremen was employed in its construction. It was unbelievably ornate and costly. The holy of holies—a room just 30 feet square—was overlaid with $18 million worth of gold! Many of the walls were inlaid with precious jewels.

Before he began to build, Solomon told a fellow king: "I am about to build a temple for the Lord my God ... It is going to be a wonderful temple because he is a great God, greater than any other" (2 Chronicles 2:4-5, TLB). Then he asked two very significant questions: "But who can ever build him a worthy home? Not even the highest heaven would be beautiful enough! And who am I to be allowed to build a temple for God?" (v. 6, TLB). If no one could build a home big enough and beautiful enough to house God, then why should the Temple be built? He gives the logical answer in these words: "But it will be a place to worship him" (ibid.).

When the building was completed a service of dedication was held. The king prayed this prayer:

> The Lord has said that he would live
>   in the thick darkness,
> But I have made a Temple for you,
>   O Lord, to live in forever!
>   *(2 Chronicles 6:1-2, TLB).*

Suddenly the glory of the Lord filled the Temple and the people fell on their faces "and worshiped and thanked the Lord" (7:3, TLB). This was a clear indication that God was at home in His house and had accepted their worship.

Since that time God's people have worshiped Him in temples and church buildings. The early Christians kept up this practice. Acts 2:46 records the fact that "they worshiped together regularly at the Temple each day" (TLB). In the next chapter we find Peter and John going to the Temple to participate in the three o'clock prayer service.

However, early in the life of the New Testament Church two clear concepts began to emerge.

1. *Worship was primary—the place of worship was secondary.* The word "together" in Acts 2:46 is the key word, not "Temple." In addition to going to the "church," they also "met in small groups . . . for Communion" (ibid.). Before long, Christians were forced to start house churches when they were not permitted to worship in the Temple. They found it was absolutely essential to gather for worship, but it was not necessary

to meet in elaborate buildings. God met with them wherever they came together.

This is still true. The church is a community of believers. We gather strength from our fellow Christians. The Body can function effectively only in togetherness. This is the genius of the church. Small wonder that Hebrews 10:25 admonishes, "Let us not give up meeting together, as some are in the habit of doing." Church leaders John Wesley and John Calvin were poles apart in some areas of theology, but they agreed on this principle. Calvin said that no man could have God as Father who did not have the Church as "mother."

The Old Testament Temple still issues a timeless call to worship to all New Testament Christians, regardless of the fact that our places of meeting are far less elaborate than Solomon's Temple.

2. *Gathering for worship prepares the church to scatter for ministry.* In the Old Testament, worship was an end in itself. But after Pentecost it became a means to the end of ministry. In his lectures at Nazarene Theological Seminary, Elton Trueblood pointed out that when Jesus left the synagogue in Nazareth, He started something new in religion—"he called unto him the twelve, and *began to send them forth*" (Mark 6:7, KJV, italics added). Before this the Temple was *centripetal*— everything was directed toward the inside. But Christ changed all that. Now His Church became *centrifugal*—it concentrated its efforts on reaching out.

This must still be the major thrust of the Church. Our Great Commission is to "go and make disciples" (Matthew 28:19). Anything less than this is less than New Testament Christianity. More and more churches no longer call their Sunday gatherings "services." They are termed "celebrations" or "worship hours." The bulletin clearly states that following the benediction the congregation leaves to begin its service.

Bill Gaither captures this concept in his gospel song "I Will Serve Thee Because I Love Thee." Worship fans the flame of loving devotion to our Lord. With this dynamic motivation we will go out to render dedicated service for Him.

No, the Church is not a building. The New Testament makes it clear that it is a Body which is housed in all kinds of buildings. All members of the Body are important and all have spiritual gifts and functions (1 Corinthians 12:12-26).

What is so special about the Church? It is a living, breathing Body of believers which is alive and well in a sick world.

The Family of God

This is something which is very special about the Church. To understand this concept we have to go all the way back to Abraham. In Genesis chapter 17 God made a covenant with him. He changed his name from Abram to Abraham which literally meant "Father of Nations" (v. 5, TLB). The Lord promised him millions of descendants who would receive His special favor. Abraham's grandson, Jacob, would be renamed Israel, and the generations which followed would be known as the "children of Israel." They were God's chosen people—His family. All others were Gentiles—outsiders, not family members.

The Church is the new family of God. Entrance comes by spiritual, not natural, birth. Jesus said to Nicodemus, "You must be born again" (John 3:7). Both Jews and Gentiles are eligible for membership in the family, for "whoever believes in him [Christ] shall . . . have eternal life" (v. 16).

Paul verifies this fact in 1 Corinthians 12:13, "For we were all baptized by one Spirit into one body—whether Jews or Greeks." He uses several new terms to characterize the new family—"the household of faith" (Galatians 6:10, KJV) and "the household of God" (Ephesians 2:19, KJV). Family members become brethren or "brothers" (Romans 12:1).

All of this points up the warm, supportive relationship which exists in the Church. Members of the family of God often have more in common with fellow believers than they do with their natural families. The New Testament word which characterizes this beautiful relationship is *koinonia* or "fellowship"

(Acts 2:42). This has to be one of the greatest benefits and blessings of family membership.

What is so special about the Church? All of this plus much more. An anonymous author put it this way:

> *I am the church. I am not perfect,*
> *for though I represent a perfect God*
> *My reins are held by imperfect man.*
> *But my great steeples point to heaven,*
> *and my crosses point to eternity.*
> *And the message preached to my people*
> *points to salvation.*
> *And my efforts are not in vain; for sometimes*
> *one man enters my doors*
> *And a new man later leaves.*

Chapter 3

Wesley Who?

by Howard Snyder

*Background Scripture: Matthew 10:7-8; 1 Thessa-
lonians 2:4-8, 10-12*

I HAVE BEEN STRUCK in recent years by the Church's growing rediscovery of how relevant John Wesley is today. You can hardly pick up a book by an evangelical author without finding some reference to him. When contemporary writers wish to point out that evangelicals have historically had a social conscience, they cite Wesley.

When the need for simple gospel preaching is emphasized, Wesley is given as an example. The fact is that Wesley illustrates several qualities that are essential for Christian faithfulness in techno-urban society. I would like to deal with these in this chapter.

Wherein lies the relevance of John Wesley for the contemporary Church? What were the factors that accounted for his impact?

Of the many factors which could be cited, six are especially relevant for today. Three of these relate to Wesley's message and three to his method.

John Wesley's Message

John Wesley had a message, and he was not ashamed of it. Wesley had something definite and specific to communicate, and the message was communicable in human language—a fact which needs emphasizing in our age. What were the principal elements of this message?

1. *A clear proclamation of the fact of personal salvation through Jesus Christ.* Wesley's message was salvation by faith. He emphasized the basic biblical teachings of man's sin and lostness, Christ's sacrifice and resurrection, and the transformation of the new birth.

There were those in Wesley's day who said such a message was no longer relevant. People would not listen. But the public response to his preaching undermined the critics. People listened and responded by the thousands.

We must emphasize that Wesley's was a *clear* proclamation of the basic gospel. Though an Oxford scholar, he had no patience with high-sounding phrases that failed to communicate. It is said that Wesley would often preach newly prepared sermons to his maid, a simple, uneducated girl, and have her stop him whenever she did not understand his words. His passion was to communicate with the masses.

This was the same Wesley who, preaching at Oxford, might quote from Latin authors or from the Greek New Testament. Wesley was a scholar, but he put his scholarship at the service of the people.

2. *A consistent emphasis on the Spirit-filled life.* Wesley constantly emphasized the need for the filling and continuing ministry of the Holy Spirit in the life of the believer, and thousands of early Methodists found the experience a reality. In nearly every city he visited, Wesley carefully examined the members of the Methodist societies about their Christian experience. Although he frequently found spiritual counterfeits, he also found much spiritual reality and power. The Holy Spirit was at work.

Wesley emphasized much more than merely a crisis experience of the infilling of the Spirit. His preoccupation was that of

Paul: Christian maturity, the edification of the Church, the forming of the stature of Christ in each believer. With Wesley there was a constant concern for Christian nurture and growth through the work of the Spirit.

3. *An active and involved social consciousness.* Wesley was supremely an evangelist. And yet, read through a list of his sermon titles or of the pamphlets he published. His topics include wealth, national sins, war, education, medical ethics, the Stamp Act, trade with North America, responsibility to the king, the liquor industry.

There was no question where Wesley stood on poverty and riches, sea piracy, smuggling, the slave trade, and other crucial issues of his day. Nor did he think he was compromising his call as an evangelist when he preached on these issues on Sunday morning. He saw, as had the Old Testament prophets, that biblical faith touches every area of life and makes everyone morally responsible, from king to collier.

And the amazing thing is that Wesley's social concern brought results. Why? First, because he awakened a new moral consciousness in the nation. Second, because others followed his example. Third, because as an effective evangelist he was instrumental in transforming thousands of lives. He instilled in his converts the same social concern, thus broadening the popular base for social reform. He proved what the history of the Church in other times and places shows: There is no combination more potent in transforming society than biblical evangelism coupled with biblical social concern—the joining of Old Testament prophet and New Testament evangelist.

Wesley himself did more than just talk about social reform. Among other things, he agitated for prison, liquor, and labor reform; set up loan funds for the poor; campaigned against the slave trade and smuggling; opened a dispensary and gave medicines to the poor; worked to solve unemployment; and personally gave away considerable sums of money to persons in need.

John Wesley's Method

But John Wesley's message is only part of the story. He saw—or rather, learned—that the clearest, most biblical proclamation of the gospel often has little effect if it is locked within the walls (literal or figurative) of the institutional church. And it is here that Wesley becomes especially relevant for the problem of wineskins.

Others before and since have preached as clearly and effectively as Wesley, but with not half the abiding results. Why? In part, because their message was encrusted in rigid, unbiblical ideas about the nature of the Church.

Wesley started out strictly "high church" in his ecclesiology, but God did not let him stay there. To a considerable degree he was still a high churchman at his death, but in many ways he learned to be remarkably flexible and unconventional. This can be illustrated by three aspects of Wesley's ministry:

1. *He did not restrict himself to the institutional church.* John Wesley's effectiveness dates from the time he began carrying the gospel outside the four walls of the church.

It happened like this: Wesley's friend, the evangelist George Whitefield, had a large congregation of coal miners at Kingswood, near Bristol, where Whitefield was preaching regularly. Whitefield's ministry was "field preaching"—assembling a large crowd in an open field and there opening the Word. Wesley frowned on this at first, for he had been, in his words, "so tenacious of every point relating to decency and order that I should have thought the saving of souls a sin if it had not been done in the church."

Whitefield requested—practically insisted—that Wesley take over his congregation so he could return to America. Wesley did not want to accept it, but after seeing Whitefield's ministry, he felt the call was from God: "At four in the afternoon, I submitted to be more vile, and proclaimed in the highways the glad tidings of salvation, speaking from an eminence in a ground adjoining to the city, to about three thousand people."

The crowds grew, and soon there were congregations in other places—in fact, within a few years, throughout England, Scotland, and Ireland. Wesley had discovered that when the people stop coming to the church, it is time for the church to go to the people.

Wesley, his brother Charles, and Whitefield did not win popular praise for their efforts. Bishop Leslie R. Marston notes, "These three men were called mad enthusiasts because they would free the gospel from the confining gothic arches of established religion and release it to the masses in street and field, to the sick and unclean in hovel and gutter, to the wretched and condemned in Bedlam and prison."

Wesley was a devout churchman. He had no intention of founding a new dissenting group; he urged his hearers and new converts to attend the regular Anglican services. He never preached in a field or marketplace at the same hour as stated worship services.

But Wesley was also a realist. He saw that many people simply would not attend the traditional church services, and even those who did failed to receive there all the spiritual help they needed. And this leads us to the second aspect of Wesley's method.

2. *He created new and workable structures for worship.* One of the first things Wesley did with his converts was to divide them into groups of a dozen, each group with its own leader. These were the famous Wesleyan "class meetings." Wesley soon discovered the spiritual dynamic of this small-group structure.

He said in 1742,

> I appointed several earnest and sensible men to meet me, to whom I showed the great difficulty I had long found of knowing the people who desired to be under my care. After much discourse, they all agreed there could be no better way to come to a sure, thorough knowledge of each person than to divide them into classes, like those at Bristol, under the inspection of those in whom I could most confide. This was the origin of our classes in London, for which I can never sufficiently praise God, the unspeakable usefulness of the institution having ever since been more and more manifest.

We have already seen how Wesley later commented that through such small-group participation his followers "began to 'bear one another's burdens' and naturally to 'care for each other,'" coming to an experiential knowledge of genuine Christian fellowship.

Wesley innovated in other aspects of church structure as well—lay ministers (thus providing for the exercise of spiritual gifts), unpretentious "preaching houses," and so forth. He felt free to make such innovations because he conceived of Methodism not as a new denomination but merely as a society within the Anglican church. But regardless of the reasons, he was one of the great innovators in church structure.

Wesley's efforts along this line say much to the contemporary church. Trapped in rigid institutional patterns, today's traditional churches too seldom experience that fellowship of the Holy Spirit of which the New Testament speaks. This was also true of 18th-century Anglicanism—and Wesley did something about it.

3. *He preached the gospel to the poor.* One of the most crucial signs of the Kingdom is *to whom* the gospel is being ministered. John Wesley, like Jesus, preached to the poor. He sought out those whom no one else was seeking.

Reading his *Journal,* one is impressed with how many times Wesley preached at 5 A.M. or a midmorning in the marketplace. Why did he often preach at five o'clock? Not for *his* convenience, but for the convenience of the laboring men and women who went to work in mine or factory at daybreak. Wesley assembled the coal miners in the fields before they started work or the crowds in the marketplace at midday. His passion was to preach the gospel to the poor, and among them he had his greatest response.

In short, John Wesley had a message, and he did not muffle it behind stained glass. He went outside the structured church, preaching the gospel to the poor. He refused to allow newborn babes to die of spiritual malnutrition, but provided spiritual homes and foster parents for them. He created new forms of the church—new wineskins—for those who responded. He matched a biblical message with methods in harmony with a biblical ecclesiology.

John Wesley's Secret

Was there one special secret behind Wesley's impact? How did Wesley "happen" to find this happy marriage of message and method?

We face here, of course, the mystery of the sovereignty of the Holy Spirit. But we can see at least some of the ways the Spirit worked in Wesley's life.

Wesley was not primarily a theologian, although he was theologically competent. He "theologized" sufficiently to find biblical answers to the basic questions of Christian experience and to confront social issues with biblical revelation. But he never worked out a consistent theological system. His theology was a mixture of high-church traditionalism, believers' church pietism, and evangelistic pragmatism. On some questions, such as infant baptism, he never worked out a consistent position but held seemingly contradictory opinions.

There is not even unanimous agreement about whether Wesley was, at heart, an Arminian or a Calvinist! If he cannot be neatly classified, it is because he sought to be thoroughly biblical.

So John Wesley's secret did not lie primarily in his theological attainments. It was not essentially theological in this sense. *But it was essentially biblical.* Wesley, the scholar, the author and editor of many books, was "a man of one book"—the Bible. He accepted it implicitly and practiced it consciously. This was his secret: the Word of God.

Wesley held the common-sense view that if the Bible is true, it will show itself true in valid human experience. So his points of reference were, first the Bible, and secondarily, experience and reason. These were his measures, not church tradition, contemporary philosophy, or the opinions of others. What the Bible said was true, regardless of what others thought, and would prove true in human living.

Because he was biblical, Wesley was free to be radical—radical in the proper sense of going back to the roots.

Not that Wesley was without his faults. He was considered by some as somewhat of an anti-Catholic bigot, although his personal relations with individual Catholics were above reproach. Some will choke on the fact that Wesley was a promonarchy political conservative with little patience for upstart American revolutionary radicals, although he sympathized with the colonists at first. But in spite of whatever criticisms are leveled against him, Wesley was at heart a Christian, as all who knew him well testified, and his faith was firmly, radically biblical.

Each age is unique—but not totally. We can learn much from the past, and especially is this true with regard to the life and structure of the church. There are few periods in the church's past as relevant for today as Wesley's England. And there, too, we find a model of some significance for testing the view of the Church and church structure.

Chapter 4

Is God on Stage?

by Ben Patterson

Background Scripture: Psalm 100:1-4; Matthew 18:19-20

THE DIFFERENCE between a biblical and a pagan understanding of worship lies in the difference between a verb and a noun. For the person of the Bible, worship is something you *do*. For the pagan, worship is a state of being.

What is it, then, we do when we ascribe worth to God and bow down and serve Him on Sunday morning? I believe we engage in a ritual drama. By ritual, I mean we use certain fixed forms of words, such as sermons, prayers, hymns. By drama, I mean that the telling of a story is woven throughout those rituals: the story of God's mighty acts of salvation in Jesus Christ.

Let me give you an example of what I mean from popular culture. When we worship God, we do essentially the same thing I did when I watched on television, for the 11th time, a replay of USC's great 1974 victory over Notre Dame. For those of you who are unfamiliar with this bit of *Heilsgeschichte* (sacred history), that was the game in which USC was down 17 points at halftime. Anthony Davis of USC received the second half kickoff one yard in his own end zone and ran it back 101 yards for a touchdown. For the rest of the second half USC totally dominated Notre Dame with Davis's runs and Pat Haden's passes to J. K. McKay. The final score: USC 55, Notre Dame 24.

"But," you protest, "you know everything that is going to happen. Why have you watched it so many times?" My answer: That is precisely the point. I watch it over and over again because I know what will happen. Certain values I have are confirmed and reaffirmed. Once again, good triumphs over evil, light over darkness.

You do the same thing whenever you watch your favorite television program. Dramatized, in story form, will be certain values and beliefs you hold to as an American. They will be about life and what it means, its problems and its solutions. Some social analysts call popular television programs, especially the interminable series variety, ritual drama. That's because they, like my favorite USC/Notre Dame game, reaffirm what we believe. They are like worship services. For many Americans they are worship services in that they are weekly, and sometimes daily, confirmations and reaffirmations of the core of values we hold in common as citizens of this country.

The Bible is filled with ritual drama. Revelation 5:9-10 is a good case in point. The multitudes of heaven are gathered around the throne of God. At His right hand stands the Lamb who has just been declared worthy to take the scroll in God's right hand and open it up. The scroll is of immense importance because it contains the decrees of God for the future of the planet Earth. The occasion is one of great joy for the congregation of heaven, so they break into a service of worship of the Lamb.

Ritual drama: That is what we are witnessing in this spectacular heavenly worship service. The story of salvation is retold and its values upheld, all as the worshipers offer thanks and praise.

A pivotal question must be asked here, the answer to which takes us to the heart of what happens in truly Christian worship. In this ritual drama, who is the audience and who is the performer? Clearly, the answer is that God is the audience and the congregation is the performer. As Soren Kierkegaard put it, in Christian worship God is the audience, the congregation the performer, and the minister, choir, and other leaders are the prompters.

If just this one fundamental truth were to sink into the consciousness of Christians, worship would be transformed. The overwhelming majority of Christian congregations have the roles reversed. The congregation regards itself as the audience, while regarding the prompters and God, I suspect, as the performers. The congregation comes to have a "worship experience." That is not only idolatrous in its reversal of worship roles, but pagan in its understanding of worship itself. Worship then becomes a noun, a state of being, an experience induced by God or the choir or the pastor. Biblically, however, worship is a verb, something the congregation or performer does.

At least three implications flow out of this understanding of worship as ritual drama. The first has to do with history. God is the God of history: of the past, the present, and the future. The Lamb *was* slain and *has made* us free, and we *shall* reign, say the words of the hymn in the Revelation passage.

Christian worship is essentially an act of remembrance. That is what the Lord's Supper does. It remembers the Lord's death, even as it celebrates His resurrection presence and looks forward to His return. There they are again: past, present, and future.

One of the fallacies and conceits of our times is that God has done little or nothing since the death of the last apostle until right now. We place great stock in the New Testament and first-century Church, and in our own. In my congregation there are those who want to sing only the new songs and those who want to sing only the old songs. What is funny about all this is that the "old songs," at their oldest, may date back to 19th-century revivalism.

The God of past, present, and future whom we worship in ritual drama was just as active in the 4th, 11th, or 17th centuries as He is now. Our songs, prayers, sermons, and confessions should recognize this in worship. Besides making us a more biblical people, it would give us a perspective on ourselves and relieve us of a bit of our conceit.

The second implication has to do with preparation. Because we are the performers, we must come to worship prepared. Can you imagine your chagrin if you paid $20.00 to hear a performance of Beethoven's Seventh Symphony and the orchestra came into the concert hall late? What if the director stood before the audience and said something like this: "Wow! Have we had a busy month! Lots of travel, several recording sessions, and now here we are, and we haven't had a chance to rehearse tonight's concert. Listen, I have a great idea. Everyone here is an accomplished musician. What do you say we just have a jam session for the next 90 minutes? Just let it flow. Be spontaneous!"

You would be angry if the orchestra arrived late and unprepared because you paid a lot of money for the performance. What did God pay for our performance? The blood of His own Son. What does this mean pragmatically? It means things like a good night's sleep on Saturday. It means things like arriving on time. I believe Sunday morning tardiness is a theological issue. It means things like prayer and Bible study on the days leading up to Sunday morning. Howard Rice has said that Reformation worship assumed of the congregation that its individual members had spent an hour a day through the week in Bible reading and prayer!

All of this contradicts what Tom Howard calls the "myth of spontaneity." It is a very appealing myth. It says we would all be free, direct, and spontaneous if we could just dismantle tradition, structures, and conventions. Unfortunately this contradicts everything else we know in human experience. It was hard work, austerity, and discipline that produced the *Dialogues* of Plato, the B Minor Mass, and the theory of relativity. Should it be any different in our relationship to God? Just as not much that is worthy, substantial, and noteworthy proceeds from mere spontaneity in other forms of human endeavor, so it is in Christian worship. I believe God is, at the very least, unimpressed with merely spontaneous worshipers.

A good metaphor for the true freedom of disciplined Christian worship can be found in the athlete's art. Nothing looks more free and spontaneous than a great athlete performing. But beneath all of that freedom and spontaneity are years of drills, repetition, sweat, strain, and more drills.

Sunday morning worship is to the rest of our lives what cultivation is to a garden. We weed, prune, water, and feed to the end that the garden may be beautiful—spontaneous gardens are not; disciplined gardens are.

The last implication has to do with focus. And with this I close, because it sums up everything. Christ is at the center of Christian worship, not us and our experience. We are not there to get, but to give. The question we should be asking ourselves on the way home on Sunday morning is not, "What did I get out of it?" but rather, "How did I do?" For when all the sermons have been preached, all the anthems sung, all the worship renewal workshops conducted, and all our innovations come and gone, that is all that will have mattered: that we said with our whole being, "Worthy is the Lamb who was slain, to receive power and wealth and wisdom and might and honor and glory and blessing!" (Revelation 5:12, RSV).

Chapter 5

Hey, Does Anyone Know Where We're Going?

by Lyle Schaller

*Background Scripture: Matthew 28:19-20; Mark
10:42-45*

PASTOR, it has been over a year since you were out to see
me. Dr. Franklin used to stop in every few weeks when he was
our minister." These words were spoken by a tiny, white-haired
widow as she stopped at the door to shake hands with her
pastor at St. John's Church.

"Thanks for reminding me," smiled Richard Hanson. "I'll
stop by the first chance I get, and we'll have a good visit. It may
not be for a while though," he warned. "You know we're pretty
busy trying to strengthen the church's outreach in this community."

The minister continued to greet his flock as they filed past
him. He exchanged brief pleasantries with most of them and
made mental notes as he was told of a member who was enter-
ing the hospital on Monday, that a light bulb was burned out in
the ladies' rest room, and that the Greens wanted their baby
baptized the second Sunday of the next month.

The last person to shake his hand that morning was Mrs.

Rogers, a tall, stately woman whose late husband had been one of the pillars of the church for over 30 years. "Good morning, Pastor," she said. "I hear you now have nearly 100 young people coming out for this new Sunday evening program you started last fall. Is that true?"

"Yes, it is true," he replied with a heartfelt smile. "Our attendance actually averages about 70 to 80, but there are over 100 young people involved." As he offered this response, Pastor Hanson felt a sense of delight that one of the "old guard" recognized what an effort was involved in developing a program that could attract 100 senior high youngsters. This warm glow suddenly disappeared when Mrs. Rogers dropped his hand with the comment, "Hrumpf, if you have 100 teenagers in this Sunday evening affair, you must be letting in a lot of outsiders! There aren't more than 30 or 40 young people that age in this congregation."

As Mrs. Rogers swept on out to the parking lot, Dick Hanson asked himself for the hundredth time, "What am I doing here?" Three years earlier he had accepted a call to St. John's. His first two pastorates after graduating from seminary had been in stable churches in smaller cities, and, while he felt he had served acceptably in both of them, after 12 years in the ministry he was ready for a new challenge when the call came from St. John's.

St. John's was the third oldest Protestant church in the state capital and for decades had been one of the leading churches in the district. The membership had dropped from over 1,500 back in the 1920s to a reported 485 over 40 years later. Some of the old-timers claimed they used to have over 1,000 persons in Sunday School every Sunday. Now the Sunday School attendance averaged fewer than 100.

The pulpit committee had been very frank about these facts; they had described the changes that had taken place in the neighborhood during the past few years. "We're looking for a minister who has had 10 to 15 years' experience, but who is young enough in age and spirit to lead us in mission in this neighborhood. Many of our members are getting along in years; most of them no longer live in this neighborhood, but they all love St. John's. They all want to see St. John's provide the ministry that is needed in this neighborhood."

Mr. Rogers, who died three weeks after Dick Hanson accepted the call to St. John's, was a member of that pulpit committee. Dick remembered his saying, "We want a minister who can come in and build up this congregation to what it used to be. There are hundreds of unchurched people living in this neighborhood. St. John's needs to go out and reach them."

Dick also recalled another member adding, "There's a lot of potential in our own congregation. If the minister would get out and call among the members and stir them up, they would attend more often and be more active."

After visiting the church and two more meetings with the pulpit committee Dick Hanson decided this was the challenge he had been seeking and accepted the call to St. John's. The first year had been the traditional honeymoon period as he called on the members, became acquainted with the leaders of the parish, and talked about the possibilities of serving the neighborhood.

Shortly before the beginning of the second year, he had outlined to the church council a new program directed toward neighborhood residents. The council had given its enthusiastic approval and in three weeks had raised the extra $4,600 he suggested was needed to carry out the program. Most of the money was allocated for the salary of a seminary student who would be full-time during the summer and would help on weekends during the school year with the youth program.

Now, after three years, what was the result? As he asked himself this question, Pastor Hanson thought perhaps it was all symbolized in a recent incident that involved the new sign in front of the church. Back in the middle of his first year as pastor, Dick had casually remarked one evening at church council that a stranger would not know what kind of church this was or the time of service. Sometime earlier during a cleanup campaign the old decrepit sign in the yard of the church had been torn down and never replaced. Six weeks after the new pastor had dropped his casual hint, a new illuminated masonry sign costing $2,000 was under construction, and every nickel of the cost was in the treasurer's hands as the result of a quiet fund-raising drive conducted by two of the men on the council.

Last Tuesday evening the district missions executive had come to meet with the congregation. He had arrived early, and since it was a warm evening, he had stood out in front talking with a couple of the members he had known for years. While they talked, one of the ladies exclaimed, "Look at those kids climbing all over the church sign! They shouldn't be allowed to do that. Why, there's even one crawling into the fellowship hall through a window! I don't know what's going to happen here." Turning to the district mission executive, she continued, "I guess now you can see why a lot of us are unhappy at how things have been going here for the past several months."

"I think I know what you mean," responded the denominational executive, "but it seems to me this is a sign of progress. I've been coming here at least once a year for nearly a decade now, and this is the first time I have seen a youngster anywhere near the church. This is progress!"

Later when he heard this story, Dick Hanson said to the district official, "This illustrates my frustrations. When I accepted a call here, it was with the clear-cut understanding that St. John's would make a major effort to serve the people living in this neighborhood. During the past two years we have reached a lot of people in the neighborhood, especially kids. So what is the result? I am criticized because I don't call in the homes of the members. The people from the neighborhood who come near the building are made to feel like they are intruders or vandals. The church treasurer has warned me that the money probably won't be available next year to hire a part-time seminary student; yet plans are moving ahead to raise $30,000 to replace the old organ. Several people have gone out of their way to point out that while we are in contact with many neighborhood residents, only a few have joined the church, and none of them are good supporters of the budget. I hear a lot more about the cost of replacing a few broken windows and repairing a couple of tables than I do about the number of youth in our Sunday evening fellowship group.

"Everyone continues to say that they want the church to serve this neighborhood," continued the pastor, "but most of them are unwilling to accept the consequences of this decision. I can't help wondering if I have made a mistake in the way I have acted. The tension is so thick in this church that you can cut it with a knife. A parish that is doing the Lord's work ought not to be torn by dissension the way this one is!"

"You're right," agreed the district executive. "When a parish is doing what it should be doing, there ought not to be the tension and conflict you describe. Yet your situation is not at all uncommon, especially in a gathered congregation such as this one. Any attempt by a gathered congregation to initiate a new ministry into the neighborhood almost invariably places the pastor in a tension-producing dilemma."

As Dick Hanson and the district executive continued their conversation, it became apparent that they were discussing two different, but closely related, problems at St. John's. The more highly visible one was the dissension in the parish and the growing tension produced by the effort to develop an effective neighborhood-oriented ministry.

The second problem at St. John's, and perhaps the basic cause of the first, was the last of a clearly defined purpose. The members had not been challenged to think carefully through the reasons for St. John's existence. Many did not see the relationship of this new effort to serve the neighborhood to the rest of the church program.

St. John's is not alone in being confronted with these two related problems. Both are disruptive and can greatly inhibit the effectiveness of the local church. Both are often neglected and eventually may develop into fatal illnesses.

Sources of Tension over Purpose

At St. John's, as happens so often in similar situations, the decision to undertake a new neighborhood-oriented ministry places the minister unexpectedly in a tension-filled dilemma. He finds himself caught between the expectations of those who believe the pastor should minister to his flock and those who have caught the new vision of the church's ministry to the world.

The source of the tension at St. John's was a result of the lack of a clear understanding of the purpose of the church. Many of the members acted on the assumption that the local church should direct its efforts toward serving the members. This meant that the pastor should be concerned *primarily* with ministering to the members. "After all, we pay his salary. Why shouldn't he be expected to give first priority to the wants and needs of the members?"

Others recognized the need for the church to reach out and serve the newcomers to the neighborhood around the church building. It appeared, however, that these members hoped this could be accomplished without making any changes at St. John's. They appeared to expect that somehow the newcomers would happily fit into the traditional pattern of the operation at St. John's. They really were not so much interested in reaching the unchurched with the gospel as they were in finding replacements for the members who died or moved away.

Another group sincerely wanted the newcomers to the neighborhood to come to St. John's, but they felt that the responsibility for this rested on the new residents, not on the members at St. John's. "Our door is wide open; we have plenty of room, and these people know they are welcome. If they want the church, all they have to do is walk in."

The result was that the more effort Pastor Hanson put into doing what he believed he had been called to do and what he believed he should be doing, the greater the tension in the parish.

The primary source of this tension was the failure of the members to have a common understanding of the reason for the existence of their church.

Closely related to the first source was the second source of tension. This was the lack of adequate lines of communication within the congregation which would enable the members to understand the purpose, to share in the development of a strategy for fulfilling that purpose, and to know what their church was doing and why. The best method of communication, of course, is participation and involvement. While this is not the primary reason, it is a very important reason for maximizing the number of people who are involved in these discussions.

A third source of tension in many parishes also grows out of this question of purpose. This is the tension that is created by a conflict between what the Lord is calling the church to do and what some members would like to see their church be. For example, one can find parishes in which a few members are attempting to manipulate the purpose and program of a parish for their own self-gratification. They may want to evaluate their church by the prestige of the members, the rate of growth, the size of the budget, the amount of the endowment, or the splendor of the building. When such standards of evaluation are applied, this will produce almost inevitably a distorted sense of purpose.

Outline for Defining Purpose

The members of each parish must make the effort to discover and articulate the purpose of their church for themselves. They can and should turn to the New Testament for the foundation on which to build their own statement of purpose.

A simplified outline can be built around three points.

1. *Congregational Care*

Here are grouped those items which are entirely or largely member-oriented. Typically this includes corporate worship, administration of the sacraments, pastoral care, fellowship, and the nurture, education, and training for Christian discipleship of the members.

2. *Outreach and Evangelism*

This part of the statement focuses on the imperative to go out and confront individuals outside the church with the good news that Jesus Christ is their Redeemer and Savior. While the first part of this outline was directed toward the parish's ministry to persons inside the gathered community, this part of the outline emphasizes the parish's responsibility to *individuals outside* the church.

43

3. *Witness and Mission*

The emphasis here is on the church's responsibility to be a living witness to Christ in the world to the groups, organizations, structures, and institutions outside the church in the world. This also helps the members to understand both the legitimacy and the imperative for the parish's involvement in the social, economic, and political issues in the local community. In part two of this outline the thrust is on Christianizing the world; in this part the emphasis is on humanizing the society in which man lives.

This three-point outline also can be used to submit to the members a "performance budget" of the church's expenditures. Instead of presenting a budget or a record of expenditures using the traditional categories of salaries, utilities, etc., these three categories are used. Instead of placing the emphasis on "input," as is done in the traditional budget, the emphasis is placed on "output" or results or program. This enables the members to see the results of the dollar input into their parish. This type of outline of purpose also encourages members to give the appropriate emphasis to all elements of purpose.

Importance of a Balanced Definition

This matter of a *balanced* statement of purpose is sometimes overlooked when a parish begins to develop a strategy for mission.

"I believe there is a middle ground here," the district executive told Dick Hanson, "and I think I can help a congregation see the legitimacy of congregational care *and* the necessity of mission and witness *and* the need for evangelistic outreach to the unchurched. The danger we run into is that a congregation overemphasizes one and neglects the other two. This can kill the church. We have had literally hundreds of Protestant parishes commit suicide by overemphasizing this matter of congregational care. They become so wrapped up in themselves that they completely, or almost completely, neglect the second and third parts of this threefold definition—evangelism and mission. Usually what happens is that this shift in emphasis occurs so gradually that no one realizes it until long after it has happened and the parish is no longer a *religious* institution but simply another institution concerned with the institutional goals of self-preservation and institutional maintenance. Churches that drift off into this distorted definition of purpose may continue to exist long after they have died as *religious* institutions. They can exist on the accumulated assets from the past from building, endowment, loyalty, tradition, and habit. They cannot witness and reach out effectively without the current income that comes only from faith, obedience to the call of the Lord, participation in the world, and love of neighbor."

Change and the Reaction to Change

"Perhaps I am sounding impatient again," said Dick Hanson, "but how long does this take? I've been here at St. John's for three years now. When I accepted the call to come here, I thought they already had made up their mind that they wanted to develop a strong, neighborhood-oriented ministry.

"Yet when we actually move in this direction and do accomplish something, we arouse a hostile reaction in many of the members. The more progress we make, the greater the tension."

"Part of the answer to your problem lies in our view of life and of the church. Instead of eagerly looking ahead to a specific day when all the people who call themselves Christian will have a clear-cut understanding of what it means to be a disciple of Christ and a member of His Church, I find it more helpful to think of this as a pilgrimage. As we move along, some people drop out of the journey, and new faces join us. We are growing in understanding, but this is a continuing process without a clearly defined terminal point. Hopefully a parish keeps moving ahead and gaining a clearer awareness of its purpose, but pastors come and go, and no one of them can be assured that during his tenure every member will develop a perfect understanding of his role as a Christian or of the purpose of the church."

"Does this mean I'll experience frustration as long as I remain in the pastorate?" asked Dick Hanson. "Are you telling me that every pastor and parish is affected by the same tensions and conflict over purpose that plague us here at St. John's?"

"That's about right," replied the district official. "The only exception I know of is in those parishes where everyone, including the minister, has accepted a narrow definition of purpose that is centered almost entirely around this item of congregational care. Fortunately there aren't many of these left. Just remember that as long as you're moving in the right direction and as long as you're making progress, there is hope."

Chapter 6

Who Says I Have to Join the Church?

by Randall E. Davey

Background Scripture: Colossians 1:24-29; 1 Peter 2:9-10

INTERESTING QUESTION. I can actually picture the sneer on a person's face as they ask it: "Who says I have to join the church?"

In response, most decent churchgoers would mount a white stallion and attack the enemy of the Crown with any and all available quotes and statistics.

The churchgoer might first try to find in history a mutually acceptable Poohbah (bigwig, honcho, big shot) who said that all good folk must join the church.

But there's a problem.

The churchgoer wouldn't find any support in the Codes of Hammurabi. Moses talks about bulls, goats, and the wheres and whys of animal husbandry; and he inks out before writing a treatise on church membership. Paul exhorted all over the Holy Land, covering every conceivable topic from lust to laziness; but he fails to mention membership.

And with all the hoopla over separation of church and

state, I think we're safe in assuming that our government will have nothing to say on the matter.

So with lance downturned, the champion of the cause has to answer the strong-willed black knight with the answer, "No one. No one says you *have* to join the church."

With honor lost and the stallion needing feed, Champion trudges out of the jousting arena. But all is not lost. En route to the stables, Champion reckons with the real problem. The issue, thinks he, is not who *must* join the church. But, rather, the issue is who *may* join the church, and what are the consequent blessings?

Joining the church, then, should be seen as the prerogative of a believer, not a penalty to be imposed. It is simply an expression of one's interest in identifying with a given organization, and in taking their claims and beliefs to be his. Membership in any group is rarely seen as an ironclad contract with a lifetime term. But it is usually an indicator of one's interest at that particular time in life.

When we join a church, we are saying any number of things. Depending on the criteria for membership, one may be saying anything from "It sounds like a good idea to me" to "By joining this fellowship, I pledge the stewardship of all that I have and all that I am to God and His purpose."

Church membership shares some similarities with baptism, as it was seen in the early days of the Church. Christian baptism was indeed a radical step and a bold witness, particularly for orthodox Jews of the day. If a Jew converted and was baptized, his unconverted family would disown him and would, in fact, conduct his funeral and treat him as though he had actually died. Now nothing this drastic usually happens when we join the church today—at least not in most countries. But church membership is a radical statement and witness about the Christian faith. The church's testimony merges with the believer's testimony. And in identifying with the church in membership, we are claiming a place of belonging or a part of the organization as our own. And we are signifying belief in the advent, death, and resurrection of Jesus Christ.

Perhaps it's worth noting that believers in many countries, the United States included, have been influenced heavily by cultural trends which mitigate against the idea of membership. This helps us understand why many 20th-century Christians resist membership, regardless of its value as a testimony to the world.

Sociologists suggest that folks these days tend to shy away from joining most organizations. So the church takes her bumps, along with the other groups. For several years, joining was "in," and it was common for politicians to list where their name appeared on the rolls of various organizations. And that listing had value. Extra care was given to joining the "right" places and particularly the "right" churches. Now, joining is not "in," and perhaps one or two causes can be cited in explanation.

Students of human behavior explain that the United States, for example, has gone through some significant and traumatic changes in the past three decades. Prior to that time, the country enjoyed a different kind of identity. In the pre-'50s, authority was okay. Policemen were helps to the neighborhood, and the military was insurance against communism and other robbers of freedom. Government and politicians were certainly not unblemished, but they did enjoy a certain kind of respect. News leaks that reported scandalous details of folk in high places were just as apt to be squelched as spread. There were clear lines of demarcation between the haves and have-nots, and folk "knew their place" in the world.

After World War II, the scene began to change. The '50s witnessed the advent of the beatniks, rejectors of the capitalist's work ethic. They were followed by the hippies, persons who were accused of being more interested in smoking grass than in cutting it. The late '60s and early '70s were the days of marches and riots. Black rights, women's rights, gay rights, children's rights—all were headline material. The heavy emphasis on equality marked by the "Who says I have to?" mentality rapidly eroded the secure base which authority figures held.

A major insult the nation received was called Watergate. Before the eyes of the world, it became apparent that the president of the United States shared some responsibility in covering up a political crime. With impeachment imminent, Richard Nixon resigned and left the White House. Gone, too, was a big hunk of the respect the office had held in the eyes of most Americans.

Perhaps the decisive blow to "authority" was dealt during the course of the Vietnam War. The American public often felt deceived by White House press releases, and returning vets verified the public's suspicion that the war seemed without purpose. Critics of the war maintained that the Johnson administration particularly was feeding an economic war with American lives. Mistrust heightened with the escalation of the war; this mistrust evolved into a general disrespect for the military. Unfortunately, many soldiers returned home, both dead and alive, as unsung heroes. Not only had lives been lost but so had credibility.

Those highlights from recent history, sociologists contend, contributed to the general feelings of mistrust which the masses now feel toward organizations. As a result, corporations and big business are more suspect than ever before. Politicans speak to cynical crowds which complain they are merely hearing the usual rhetoric and lies.

The consequent feelings of mistrust, cynicism, withdrawal, and isolationism affects the church as well. Some even feel that the 20th-century church suffers more than other groups. These people refer to the church as a place where "intimate strangers" meet. You see, it only follows that if a person cannot trust leadership and organizations, he must rely solely upon himself.

And so it is, the problem that took root in Eden is still at work today. It was an avid interest in assuming authority and enjoying equality with God that resulted in Adam and Eve getting marched right out of the garden with an angelic escort. It was lack of interest in others and abject individualism which Paul attacked in his letter to the churches in Galatia. He warns, "For you were called to freedom, brethren; only do not turn your freedom into an opportunity for the flesh, but through love *serve one another*" (5:13, NASB, italics added).

In short, that which was a problem from the beginning of creation is still causing the Church fits today.

Helping folks understand their feelings of mistrust and withdrawal is only step one in answering Champion's good question concerning who may join the church. Another step is helping them understand that church membership is not synonymous with membership in the Body of Christ. That is, it is quite possible to belong to St. Helena's Third Church and have no relationship with Jesus Christ whatsoever. It is equally possible to be a redeemed child of God without one's name appearing on anyone's official membership roll.

The New Testament helps us realize that the Church is not a place, though we refer to certain buildings as churches. Properly, the Church refers to folk. And in its purest sense, it means folks who have responded to God's grace and gift of faith in repentance—believers who have become new creatures in Christ. The many synonyms for the Church, such as "people of God," "saints," "elect," "beloved," "called," "kingdom of priests," "a holy nation," all serve the idea that the Church is not a place but persons under God. To belong, then, is to belong to God and people—an idea as basic as the great commandment.

Paul expands the idea of belonging by comparing the Church to the Body of Christ. Every believer is a member of the Body and is gifted by God for particular functions within the Body. Ephesians 4 and a comparable passage in 1 Corinthians and Romans illustrate the simple truth that the church happens when two or more gather together in His name. The biblical concept of the "universal priesthood of believers," a Reformation phrase, adds support to the Body concept. Here, the believer learns of his identity in Christ as a minister, bridge-builder, or priest (1 Peter 2:9). As a priest of God, he is to engage in the ministry of reconciliation (2 Corinthians 5:18), presenting every man complete in Christ (Colossians 1:28). In the Body, then, one finds identity, purpose, and belonging.

Joining a church, then, is a way for a believer to ward off temptation to isolationism—an inviting idea in an impersonal, untrusting age.

Many folk gravitate to large churches simply because they can get lost in the crowd. And lost they may be. You see, it's tough to be a part of the Body of Christ while maintaining a spectator posture, like the media ministry fans.

It's also tough to find that place of belonging and ministry while roaming from one fellowship to another, avoiding commitment anywhere. And it's tough to act out your ministry and thus fulfill the will of God for the church if hobbies and secular interests squeeze regular church attendance out of your schedule. And it's tough to understand the dynamic of faith living and faith giving apart from a fellowship where the Word is proclaimed, prayers are prayed, and testimony to the reality of Christ is voiced.

Isolation, then, has no place in the Church of Jesus Christ.

The church is a place of real belonging, real identity, and real purpose. It stands in stark contrast to the idea of church as a place good people should go once or twice a week to sing a little, pray a little, and suffer through a message. Rather, it's the assembly point of many believers who share a common faith. It's the place you go and, in one sense of the word, "enter on His turf" to give Him glory and worship. It's the place where you exercise various gifts and where you go for feeding. The life of faith takes on definite learning styles as disciple-priests search the Word, meditate on it both day and night, and are taught of the Teacher, God the Holy Spirit.

Knowing this to be so, there is value in finding a place of belonging in a fellowship that has ministries across the land. In a high-tech age, many believers have occasion, often without choice, to move from one part of the country to another. The transition is difficult enough, but the blow can be softened if one has allied with a church that has a widespread ministry. Denominations enjoy that luxury. A Christian can move to a new area and immediately find a comradery with like-minded believers. There, one finds a certain sameness, a continuity or perpetuation of a ministry concept. And growth continues. Personal ministry goes uninterrupted and the believer is able to affirm that there is indeed one Lord, one Spirit, and one baptism.

Church membership is not a guarantee of eternal salvation. And denominationalism certainly doesn't rule out the possibility of error. But both have positive value and are worthy of consideration in guiding a believer to one's place in the Body of Christ.

With Champion, we must answer, "No one says you *have* to join the church. No one." And with him we affirm, "But you may."

Chapter 7

Who Took My Tithe?

by C. Neil Strait

Background Scripture: Genesis 14:17-20; Malachi 3:8-10; 2 Corinthians 8:7; 9:7

THERE IS A PRINCIPLE of giving written deep into the fabric of the Bible. Its boldest proclamation is "Will a man rob God? Yet you rob me. But you ask, 'How do we rob you?' In tithes and offerings. You are under a curse—the whole nation of you—because you are robbing me. Bring the whole tithe into the storehouse, that there may be food in my house" (Malachi 3:8-10).

Money has always been high on God's list. Now that may sound strange. But God knows, better than we do, just how much importance man attaches to money. So, God must be specific with man about money if He is going to help man develop a satisfactory relationship with Him.

God talks about tithes and offerings in His revelations to man. Tithing—the giving of 10 percent of our income to God— is not something that came to us through the Mosaic law. It is older than the code, for Abraham gave tithes to Melchizedek, as stated in Genesis 14:17-20.

The New Testament ushers in the dispensation of grace. Tithing, then, is no longer only a matter of law, but now a matter of grace. Dr. Hugh C. Benner, a Bible student and church leader in the middle 1900s, has pointed out that grace encourages obedience. And Paul says in 2 Corinthians 8:7, "Excel in this grace of giving." Paul admonishes, "Each man should give what he has decided in his heart to give, not reluctantly or under compulsion, for God loves a cheerful giver" (9:7).

Jesus left no doubt about the Law's validity in the era of grace—"Do not think that I have come to abolish the Law or the Prophets; I have not come to abolish them but to fulfill them" (Matthew 5:17).

Dr. Benner made this observation concerning giving under law and under grace: "If the tithe represented the minimum financial responsibility to God under the law, surely grace cannot imply less."[1] A thorough study of the Scriptures reveals a principle of giving written deep into the relationship between man and God. Wise is that man who gives God the benefit of the doubt and moves into the arena of tithing, obediently and optimistically.

Principles of Personal Giving

Lynn Buzzard, in an interview in *Leadership,* made this observation: "Giving is an act of turning funds over to the Lord, releasing control."[2] The "releasing control" factor is important. Too much giving is with strings attached. Real New Testament, grace-inspired giving should be free of any conditions—it is giving *to* Jesus, not giving *for* Jesus. Giving *to* the cause of Christ is release that has worship and love as its reason. Giving *for* a cause, even the cause of Christ, can be giving with strings attached, in that the end result is watched as if the dollars are still under the control of the giver.

What we need to remember in our giving is that the money really does not belong to us anyway!

What a shock, huh?

The bottom line is that all we have, or ever will have, is only on loan to us by God. Psalm 50:12 reminds us of God's ownership—"the world is mine, and all that is in it." God has entrusted into our care material things, among them money. And it is our task to be faithful stewards. Paul reinforces this with the proclamation "Now it is required that those who have been given a trust must prove faithful" (1 Corinthians 4:2). Randal Denny, a local church pastor, reminds us that the "first defection from the church was not over theology, but stewardship."[3]

Only those who believe that everything belongs to the Lord can relinquish a part of it back to Him with joy and gratitude. It is an exercise of obedience that flows out of a relationship of love. "We love because he first loved us" (1 John 4:19).

Christian stewardship is challenged in the contemporary world. Paul G. Schurman, in his book *Money Problems and Pastoral Care,* wrote: "Christian stewardship is not easy to practice. Contemporary values as reflected in the mass media are a constant source of seduction to covetousness, the idolatrous worship of money and material possessions."[4]

Our giving should be out of love with a knowledge that our debt to God can never be repaid. God has given us so much, in Christ, that our greatest gifts cannot begin to repay our debt of gratitude and love. Our giving is not to repay but to express love and gratitude.

An amazing biblical fact enters at the point of our generous, love-offered giving. The more we give, the more God gives—not necessarily materially—but of His grace, love, and presence. Luke expressed it like this: "Give, and it will be given to you. A good measure, pressed down, shaken together and running over, will be poured into your lap. For with the measure you use, it will be measured to you" (Luke 6:38).

A caution needs to be sounded. Our giving is love-based, not with an idea of receiving. If our giving is with intent to receive, then there is no love or gratitude behind the gift. Only selfishness. True giving is giving with no intent that some condition attends the gift.

Another facet to be remembered in our giving is that giving to God is the wisest investment of our human resources. That which is invested in the plan and purpose of God has a way of not only blessing the giver but bringing others into the cycle to be recipients and benefactors of our giving.

Bible student Oswald Chambers points out a fact that we need to consider in our giving. He said, "The greatest competitor of devotion to Jesus is service for Him." Do not put a dollar sign on your service for Christ and expect that to exempt you from giving. It will rob you of the joy of giving that you need to enrich your spiritual life.

Another factor to consider is the temptation to stop tithing. And there are a thousand reasons to stop tithing, but none is valid scripturally. But when the temptation comes, here is a good suggestion from writer Stephen A. Bly. Make a big poster and on it put the letters "I, _____, have stopped giving money to my church because _____." Be honest in your reason.

Then imagine yourself posting this sign where all your Christian friends could see it. Try to envision taking it to your job and posting it near where you work. Bly says, "If such a sign would hamper your ministry and witness, so would holding back funds."[5]

Church Management of the Tithe

Good planning is vital in the church's stewardship of its tithe. Just as individuals are to be responsible stewards with money, so are churches. Their special New Testament function underscores the divine mandate to handle tithes and offerings properly and with discretion.

The starting point for the church is a budget. A budget will establish the priorities for ministry and improve money management, as well as provide a periodic review toward goals achievement. A budget establishes a point of reference and gives rationale for giving. A budget is the starting point for sound fiscal responsibility.[6]

Accountability is necessary. Where does the money go? Who counts it? Who deposits it? Who writes the checks? Is there a monthly report? Where are the checks and balances? These are all good questions.

Churches are not corruption-proof. So controls and accountability factors need to be established to eliminate potential problems. Good accountability insures against practices and procedures that challenge credibility.

Proper accounting procedures are a must. A system that both properly records the income and documents the expenditures will keep a church's credibility intact. When tithes and offerings are entrusted to the treasury of a church, there should be a system worthy of the trust.

Faithful disbursements are necessary. Every cent given for a cause should eventually have a disbursement to that cause. Misappropriating funds is not accepted in the secular world, and it certainly has no place in the church.

Allocations and budgets speak volumes. Especially do they speak to the impressionable minds of youth. Author Paul Schurman says, "What is needed is a radical reassessment of the goals and basic values that we are assigning to the next generation ... The New Testament guidelines on stewardship provide a direction for such reevaluation."[7]

A church writes its history through its giving. Its concern for others is told by its checkbook. Bible student Fletcher Spruce wrote," Just as it is damaging for a man to spend all of his money on himself and forget his obligation to others, so it is damaging for a church to spend all its income at home and forget its obligation to others."[8]

Where there are surplus funds, for even a short period of time, wise and safe investments should be considered. The Lord's money should not be idle! His causes reap the benefit and blessing of the wise use and investment of resources.

The Church's Mission and Its Money

Know the cause or reason to which you give. Invest in meaningful mission. Does this imply that some causes within the church are not meaningful? It may sound heretical, but the answer is yes. We cannot assume that all causes that come before us, even in the church, are high-priority items. Gifts and offerings of love are interested in Christ's mission, and not all causes are such.

Monitor the percentages. How does the music budget compare with the children's budget? How does the missions compare to buildings? How does the youth budget compare with the maintenance budget? Percentages tell a story. And the story is often one of interest, comforts, pet projects, more than mission, ministry, and priority.

Monitor the effectiveness of the program/ministry/function. Is it fulfilling the mission for which it was designed? Does the church board, or some committee or group, have the right criteria for determining mission or purpose? How about the cost-effectiveness of the item? Is there a better way to get the same results?

Investments with Eternal Dividends

A church must invest in *people*. Dr. Phineas F. Bresee, an early leader in the Church of the Nazarene, once said, "I may take the Lord's goods, and so invest it that it shall be turned into life—personal, transfigured, saved, and glorified life, which shall make heaven more glorious." The church must make people its priority. Its budget, its giving, its programs, its ministries must reflect concerns that are people-related.

A church must invest in *needs*. True value clarification—on a regular basis—is necessary to keep the church on track. It is easy, even in a church, for wants to get in the way of needs. One of the tasks of the church is to help people clarify their values—especially their material values. And a church's response to needs is a good way to teach values.

A church must invest in God's *purposes/mission*. Theologian John Wesley saw money as an instrument for accomplishing God's purposes. The local church is bombarded with requests for money, both from within and from without. It is not easy to sort out all the requests, but it is a part of biblical stewardship. The church board must guard against giving just because someone is crusading for a cause. While it may be a genuine cause, it may not be the highest priority at the time.

A church must always be asking, "What people-related ministries and needs are most important for us at this time in our history?" David Livingstone's words are good for the church. He said, "I will set no value on anything I have or may possess except in relation to the kingdom of God."

59

Giving is one of God's ways of making Christians. Generous, unconditional giving allows God an opportunity to bless and build the believer.

Consistent tithing is your only assurance that the money God entrusts to you will have some eternal significance. It is a big dividend for such a small expenditure. And smaller, yet, when compared with what Christ gave for us.

---

1. Hugh C. Benner, "Tithing: A Divine Challenge," a tract (Kansas City: Beacon Hill Press of Kansas City, n.d.).

2. Lynn Buzzard, "War and Peace in the Local Church," *Leadership*, Summer 1983, 29.

3. Randal Earl Denny, *Where the Action Is* (Kansas City: Beacon Hill Press of Kansas City, 1981), 15.

4. Paul G. Schurman, *Money Problems and Pastoral Care* (Philadelphia: Fortress Press, 1982), 9.

5. Stephen A. Bly, "A Code of Conduct for Boards," *Leadership*, Summer 1983, 33.

6. C. Neil Strait, "A Budget Primer," *Leadership*, Spring 1981, 57.

7. Schurman, *Money Problems*, 15.

8. Fletcher Clarke Spruce, *Storehouse Tithing Enlistment Program* (Kansas City: Nazarene Publishing House, 1966), 90.

Chapter 8

So What if the Poor Don't Feel Comfortable in Our Church?

by Michael J. Christensen

Background Scripture: Matthew 25:31-46

IT SEEMS THE CHURCH has come of age. Christians are successful and church attendance is respectable. We have famous Christian athletes, affluent Christian executives, powerful Christian politicians, converted movie stars, and gospel rock artists. Today's Church identifies with winners, and it attracts the influential.

But what about the losers of the world?

Does the Church have anything to offer: the child who is always chosen last to be on the school baseball team? the teenager who is ugly and unpopular? the young adult who dropped out of college and never finds a decent job? the world's masses whose circumstances keep them on the losing side in life's struggle? Does the Church of God have a word of affirmation for the down-and-out, the poor, and the oppressed?

To answer this question, let's focus on *winning and losing,* assert the truth that *God takes sides,* and the *biblical basis* for

God's special interest, sound the call to *radical discipleship,* and apply the calling to the *mission of today's Church.*

Winning and Losing

In life, sometimes you win and sometimes you lose. Winners are those with all the breaks, who succeed in reaching their goals and come out on top. Losers are those whose cards are stacked against them, who fail to achieve life's advantages and end up last in line.

Winning and losing are a part of life. The sun of divine providence shines on the just and the unjust, and the rain falls on good and bad alike (Matthew 5:45). One who is righteous is no more likely to get rich, be powerful, or stay healthy than one who is evil. Social status, material comforts, educational breaks, good health, and freedom from struggle are basically givens. Although we do make choices in how we respond to personal circumstances, winning and losing are largely determined by heredity, environment, and chance.

The writer of Ecclesiastes observed this truth in ancient times: "I realized another thing, that in this world fast runners do not always win the races, and the brave do not always win the battles. Wise men do not always earn a living, intelligent men do not always get rich, and capable men do not always rise to high positions. Bad luck happens to everyone. You never know when your time is coming. Like birds suddenly caught in a trap, like fish caught in a net, we are trapped at some evil moment when we least expect it" (Ecclesiastes 9:11-12, TEV).

The essential question in the winning and losing game is not "Why me, Lord?" but "Where are You, God? Whose side are You on?"

God Has Favorites

The longer I live in the city and minister in neighborhoods like New York's Times Square and San Francisco's Haight-Ashbury, the more painfully aware I am of the truth that God has a special interest in one certain group of people: those who are "losers" in the world's eyes, "least" in the sight of the Church, but "greatest" in the kingdom of heaven. God has favorites—orphans, widows, and pilgrims; the despised, afflicted, and impoverished.

We live in a sinful, fallen world. Everywhere we see broken men and women, oppressed and needy children, hurting people—people desperate for the love and healing that only Christ can bring. What the Bible teaches about the Church's responsibility to these kinds of people is summed up in the simple words of Jesus: "Blessed are the poor in spirit, for theirs is the kingdom of heaven" (Matthew 5:3). A chief concern of God is for those who hurt in body, soul, and spirit. The Church is to minister to the "losers" of the world, those Christ called "the least of . . . mine" (25:40).

But doesn't God love everybody—the rich as well as the poor, the healthy as well as the sick, one must ask? The answer is yes, of course; God loves everyone equally. But this is not the issue. The issue is—on whose side is God in the struggle of existence?

It doesn't take much insight or experience to understand that life in our sinful world is a struggle between the *haves* and the *have-nots,* the powerful and the weak, the oppressors and the oppressed, the winners and the losers.

God looks down upon the arena of human struggle and is not impartial. He takes sides. And the side He takes is the side of the poor and oppressed, the downtrodden and the hopeless, the outcasts and underdogs of the world. God identifies not with winners but with losers.

Biblical Bases

We see this truth woven unmistakably through both the Old and New Testaments. There are over 300 scripture verses that speak specifically about God's special interest in poor and oppressed people. Consider the following examples.

God saw the sufferings of the children of Israel, heard their cries, and set them free (Exodus 3:7-8). God is a God of liberation! "The Lord is a refuge for the oppressed, a stronghold in times of trouble. . . . he does not ignore the cry of the afflicted" (Psalm 9:9, 12).

The Old Testament prophet Amos condemned those who

"oppress the poor and crush the needy" (4:1). He preached the same sermon long before Martin Luther King did: "But let justice roll on like a river, righteousness like a never-failing stream!" (5:24). The prophet Micah adds his insight into true religion: "He has showed you, O man, what is good. And what does the Lord require of you? To act justly and to love mercy and to walk humbly with your God" (6:8).

Isaiah was another prophetic advocate for social justice on behalf of the weak: "Seek justice, encourage the oppressed. Defend the cause of the fatherless, plead the case of the widow" (1:17). It is not enough to fast and pray inwardly, Isaiah reminds the people. True spirituality is the expression of one's faith in action and involvement in people's lives: "Is not this the kind of fasting I have chosen: to loose the chains of injustice and untie the cords of the yoke, to set the oppressed free and break every yoke? Is it not to share your food with the hungry and to provide the poor wanderer with shelter—when you see the naked, to clothe him, and not to turn away from your own flesh and blood?" (58:6-7).

The Old Testament record is clear: God is on the side of the downtrodden. God's people likewise are to identify with and help those He cares for so deeply.

The New Testament also affirms God's special-interest group. Long after the prophets, Jesus appears on the scene and preaches His first sermon in the synagogue from the Book of Isaiah: "The Spirit of the Lord is upon Me, because He anointed Me to preach the gospel to the poor. He has sent Me to proclaim release to the captives, and recovery of sight to the blind, to set free those who are downtrodden, to proclaim the favorable year of the Lord" (Luke 4:18-19, NASB).

For the rest of His earthly life He lived out that prophecy: preaching to the poor, liberating captives, healing the sick, encouraging the weak, and proclaiming the year of the Lord's favor. He was the incarnation of God's heartfelt interest in the poor and oppressed.

The Pharisees accused Jesus of being a glutton and a drunkard, a friend of sinners, prostitutes, and tax-collectors. These were the kinds of people Jesus spent much of His time with. To those who questioned why He ate, drank, and hung out with undesirables, He simply said: "It is not the healthy who need a doctor, but the sick. I have not come to call the righteous, but sinners to repentance" (Luke 5:31-32).

Radical Discipleship

What a radical Jesus was! To follow Jesus is to embrace a radical discipleship.

Someone recently asked me if I ever heard of the Four Radical Principles. After confessing that I hadn't, he quoted me the following:

1. God loves the poor and oppressed and has a radical cause for your life.
2. The visible church is too rich, sinful, selfish, powerful, capitalistic, and militaristic to know and experience God's radical cause.
3. Identification with the poor and oppressed for whom Christ died is the only provision for this sin and injustice. Active social and spiritual involvement in the lives of others is the only way to fulfill the Great Commission of Christ.
4. We must individually and corporately stand up to the principalities and powers of this oppressive age and become advocates of the poor and oppressed in order to manifest the gospel. Be sure to count the cost before proceeding to pray the prayer of conversion to discipleship.

If Jesus' heart aches for the underdogs and losers of the world, and if He has a radical cause for His disciples that involves living out the whole gospel for the whole person, then how do we fulfill this calling? What does the Word of God say to those of us who are not losers by the world's standards? More personally, what does this say to me—Michael Christensen—who was born into a good, strong, healthy, and comparatively rich family; who has succeeded in most of the things I have attempted; and who has not suffered much in life? What does the call to radical discipleship mean to me and others who consider themselves winners?

65

On one level, the gospel confronts us all with the truth: Unless you know yourself to be a loser—poor in spirit, in need of health and wholeness—there is no salvation for you. Only the sick and unrighteous need a doctor and a Savior.

On another level, the Lord meets us where we are with the challenge: "What are you doing for the least of Mine?" Since God Almighty identifies with the losers of the world, you and I also must identify with them. Since God is on the side of the poor and oppressed, so must we who call ourselves God's people, involve ourselves with those to whom justice has been denied and life has been cruel. In the same way that Christ emptied himself of His divine power and riches to become a humble servant, so must we empty ourselves of our extravagances and successes and become servants of our fellow men and women. We are called to be advocates of righteousness, champions of those who cry out for justice. This is what the Church's mission is all about—preaching and demonstrating the whole gospel for the whole person, body, soul, and spirit.

The Church's Mission

One of today's evangelical churches, the Church of the Nazarene, was born from the dream of P. F. Bresee "to have a place in the heart of the city, which could be made a center of holy fire, and where the gospel could be preached to the poor."[1] To this end, he recommended that houses of worship be "plain and cheap" so that "everything should say welcome to the poor."

This particular denomination takes its name from the fact that Jesus was from Nazareth—a ghetto comprised of losers so socially unacceptable that the people said of Jesus: "Can anything good come out of Nazareth?" (John 1:46, RSV). The mission of this church, according to the first piece of Nazarene literature ever published, is to preach the gospel to the poor "upon whom the battle of life has been sore."[2]

Christ came to offer abundant life to those who were down and despondent: "Come to me, all you who are weary and burdened, and I will give you rest" (Matthew 11:28). The Early

Church likewise reached out and ministered to the lowly and the poor. Consider the composition of the Early Church:

> "Brothers, think of what you were when you were called. Not many of you were *wise* by human standards; not many were *influential;* not many were of *noble birth.* But God chose the *foolish things* of the world to shame the wise; God chose the *weak things* of the world to shame the *strong.* He chose the *lowly things* of this world and the *despised things* ... so that no one may boast before him" *(1 Corinthians 1:26-29, italics added).*

Compare this with the kind of people we find in churches today: educated, influential, prosperous, and sophisticated. It is certainly one of the purposes of the Church to help raise people's social, economic, and educational status. But in the process, the Church often forgets her lowly origins and fails to continue preaching the gospel to the poor. Instead of providing facilities in locations in which the poor feel at home, the Church moves to more attractive quarters to attract more prosperous parishioners. In this age of Christian affluence, extravagance, and success, it is not surprising that the poor no longer feel comfortable in many of our churches.

Evangelical churches in the early 20th century attracted the poor and uneducated, the urban working class, and the rural farm laborers. Street people, orphans, widows, and neglected families were helped by members throughout the week and were entitled to a front-row seat in church on Sunday.

Although much has changed since then, our mission remains the same: to preach the gospel to the poor and demonstrate God's love in tangible ways.

The good news of Jesus Christ addresses the needs of the body, soul, and spirit. We must not set a spiritual gospel against a social gospel. There is but one good news of Jesus Christ—and it has both spiritual and social implications. The whole gospel for the whole person is both a *proclamation* that God loves us and a *manifestation* of that love through our actions.

In the words of P. F. Bresee: "We went [to Los Angeles] feeling that food and clothing and shelter were the open doors to the hearts of the unsaved poor, and that through these doors we could bear to them the life of God."[3]

Compassionate service as the door to spiritual wholeness is the gift of God through His Church. "Let the poor be fed and clothed," Bresee continues; "let us pour out of our substance for this purpose; but let us keep heaven open, that they may receive the unspeakable gift of His love, in the transforming power of the Holy Ghost."[4]

During the past 10 years I have been involved in urban missions that identify with the poor and oppressed and seek to bring Christ's healing presence to broken lives.

Golden Gate Community in San Francisco, the Lamb's Mission in New York, Community of Hope in D.C., and the Bresee Institute in Los Angeles are just a few of the significant urban ministries sponsored by my denomination.

Middle-class suburban churches can adopt the same spirit of urban ministry and preach the gospel to the poor who are to be found in every city and town.

The Church must never forget that God is on the side of the poor and the oppressed. Christianity is for "losers" in the world's eyes. You and I are responsible for how we treat people neglected by society. We are called to feed someone who is hungry, clothe someone who is needy, open up your home to someone who needs shelter, listen to someone who is lonely, and help someone who needs a friend. Only as we identify with and help those Jesus called "the least of . . . mine" can we show them that they are "winners" in God's kingdom.

---

1. William E. McCumber, "Unto the Poor the Gospel Is Preached," *Herald of Holiness* (October 1, 1983): 18.

2. Leslie Parrott, *Introducing the Nazarenes* (Kansas City: Beacon Hill Press of Kansas City, 1969).

3. McCumber, *Herald of Holiness*.

4. Ibid.

Chapter 9

Does God Require Overtime?

by Jarrell W. Garsee

Background Scripture: Matthew 25:14-30; 1 Corinthians 4:1-6

STRANGE QUESTION, isn't it? But the frantic, frenzied life-style of so many Christians makes it a valid question.

In fact, a new Christian watching a "nonstop" older Christian might be tempted to believe that the veteran's never-ceasing effort was inspired by "supposed scriptures" like:

- *Blessed are the pure in heart, for they shall be overworked.*
- *Six days shalt thou labour and do all thy work, and then on the seventh day thou shalt do all the Lord's work.*
- *Come unto me, all ye that labour and are heavy laden, and I will give you two more jobs.*
- *Greater works than these shall ye do, because ye shall work overtime.*
- *The Lord helps those who help, and help, and help.*

Fortunately, these non-scriptures exist only in the "First Epistle of Hezekiah to the Reclining Saints at Lazy Hollow."

In an honest effort to answer the question "Does God require overtime?" I want us to look at a number of principles which have a bearing on the biblical answer. No one of these principles alone will sufficiently answer the question. But once we have had a chance to review them all, we should be able to find a meaningful answer.

God expects each Christian to exercise responsible stewardship. Each Christian has received blessings (grace and forgiveness), daily guidance, and resources (time, money, abilities). In Matthew 25:14-30, Jesus explains the responsibility of a steward, and the accounting that will be made.

Stewards are to be faithful and fruitful. In 1 Corinthians 4:1-2, we are told we must be faithful (trustworthy) "stewards of the mysteries of God" (NASB). The parable of the talents makes it plain that God expects an increase from the proper use of our time, as well as our other resources.

God does not expect you to do everything. I blush when I think how, as a young and very unwise home mission pastor with 13 members, I "did everything" ... custodian, painter, grass-mower, adult Sunday School teacher, secretary, church visitor, choir director, and preacher! I did, however, allow my wife to direct the Vacation Bible School. How much better if I had "equipped" those 13 beautiful saints for the work of ministry.

The work is not being shared evenly. Some people do very little; others who are more conscientious try to compensate for their own failures.

I've heard it said the church is full of willing people: "a few willing to work, and most willing to let them." Churches are too much like football games that feature "22 men on the field who desperately need rest, and 22,000 people in the stands who desperately need exercise."

A labor stoppage may be necessary to encourage commitment from others. Until we quit trying to do it all, some of the people who think they are more "meagerly talented" will not become bold enough to take part in the ministry Christ has for them. Every member of the Body of Christ is essential in order

70

for the Church to minister effectively. A study of the beautiful analogy of the spiritual Body compared to the physical body in 1 Corinthians 12 reveals the need for everyone to be part of the ministry.

Fear motivation is not God's plan. Sometimes fear (the tool of Satan) causes us unconsciously to demand overtime of ourselves. But this is not faith or faithfulness. "God hath not given us the spirit of fear; but of power, and of love, and of a sound mind" (2 Timothy 1:7, KJV). The proper motivation for Christian service is love. Paul proclaims that "the love of Christ constraineth us" (2 Corinthians 5:14, KJV). The only motivation adequate to provide maximum spiritual impact is love from Christ, love to Christ, and love to others in Christ's name and in His power.

Burnout is not God's prescription. We hear a lot about burnout. When it happens, it is usually because we have been doing the wrong thing or too much of a good thing. And sometimes it happens because we are doing it in our own strength or for our own purposes. When Elijah faced burnout because of stress, pressure, isolation, physical fatigue, and emotional outpouring, God restored him with food, rest, new fellowship, and a new mission (1 Kings 19).

Setting priorities is important. Jesus told us to "seek first His kingdom and His righteousness; and all these things shall be added to you" (Matthew 6:33, NASB). God must be our first priority, people are next, and things are last. Love is the only thing that lasts forever, and only what is done to initiate and nurture love toward God and others will last.

Tithing your time releases you from compulsion to overwork. There are 168 hours in each week. Make a covenant to give God 10 percent of those hours. I suggest to the people in my congregation that those 16.8 hours could very profitably be spent in the following breakdown:

- Daily quiet times of prayer and Bible study   7 hours
- Sunday School, worship, evening services, prayer meeting   4 hours
- Bible study in a small group   2 hours

- Ministry in the church   2 hours
- Witnessing   1.8 hours

There really is enough time to do what we need to do if we tithe this important resource.

Procrastination damages effectiveness. Too many people seem to operate by the guideline that they should never start today what they can delay until next week. Let each of the members of your group take the enclosed "Procrastination Survey"[1] to determine level of efficiency.

Procrastination Survey

	Yes	No
1. Do you feel resentful when someone reminds you of tasks you have left undone?	____	____
2. Do you feel you have too much to do each day?	____	____
3. Do you find yourself frequently making excuses for work unfinished?	____	____
4. Do you spend time on nonessentials while letting important work go?	____	____
5. Do you sometimes delay a task so long that you're embarrassed to do it?	____	____
6. Do you use high-energy times for low-priority tasks?	____	____
7. Do you often have a hard time determining what to do first?	____	____
8. Do you often make promises—to yourself, to others, to God—and then fail to keep them?	____	____
9. Do you sometimes agree to do a task and then regret it?	____	____
10. Do you often fail to list tasks you agree to do?	____	____
11. Do you think you work better under pressure?	____	____

12. Do you put off doing your income tax form until April? _____ _____
13. Do you almost always feel in a hurry? _____ _____
14. Do you continue to work on tasks even when they are as good as they need to be? _____ _____
15. Do you sometimes think that by waiting long enough the tasks will not have to be done? _____ _____
16. Do you have difficulty saying no to people? _____ _____
17. Do you think more about the one complaint than the many compliments? _____ _____
18. Do you feel frustrated much of the time? _____ _____
19. Do you feel guilty while playing? _____ _____
20. Do you forget to write down what you agree to do? _____ _____

Give yourself five points for each *Yes* answer and total your score.
Score:

0-20	Efficiency expert
25-40	Doing well
45-60	Room for improvement
65-80	You need help
85-100	Full-blown chronic procrastinator

Some of these questions reveal that a tendency to "work overtime" for the Lord is really poor time management.

Life must be kept balanced. Dr. Karl Menninger, a specialist in mental health, says there are four necessary factors in order to maintain wholeness and health:

> ✔ Work
> ✔ Worship
> ✔ Play
> ✔ Love

Rank yourself on the "Balance Survey"[2] to determine areas of need in your life.

Are Your Life and Ministry in Balance?

Rank yourself in each of the following areas.

	Yes		Sometimes		No
1. I can relax.	1	2	3	4	5
2. It's easy for me to get to sleep at night.	1	2	3	4	5
3. I wake up in the morning feeling refreshed.	1	2	3	4	5
4. I can concentrate.	1	2	3	4	5
5. Any unexplained physical aches and pains?	1	2	3	4	5
6. I feel flat and listless.	1	2	3	4	5
7. I am an example of energy and vitality.	1	2	3	4	5
8. I can handle unexpected changes or challenges.	1	2	3	4	5
9. My family and friends have a great attitude about my life's balance.	1	2	3	4	5
10. I pay my bills regularly.	1	2	3	4	5
11. My house or apartment is usually pretty neat and clean.	1	2	3	4	5
12. I keep myself looking pretty neat and clean.	1	2	3	4	5
13. I keep my car running and looking pretty good.	1	2	3	4	5
14. I have a plan for keeping my life balanced.	1	2	3	4	5

Evaluate your responses and circle the three areas that need the most work.

Remember that recreation is vital. That's not "wreck-reation," but the essential change of pace which provides a person with renewal, revitalization, and rebuilding of reserves and resources. God's Word declares: "Though our outward man perish, yet the inward man is renewed day by day" (2 Corinthians 4:16, KJV).

Be sure your "intimate witness" is the best. I do not believe God calls us to tasks that force us to ignore and neglect our own families—spouse, parents, children, siblings—in order to work overtime in the vineyard of the Lord. Use the time, energy, sensitivity, and love necessary to do all in your power to minister effectively to those nearest you.

You may need to "schedule appointments" with your own family so they know you are serious about making them a high priority in your "Christian caring." I thank God for the time when the Spirit taught me, as a pastor, that the *maintenance needs* of my own family were to be held as a priority equal to the *emergency needs* of other people's families.

Flexibility in ministry may help you grow. Over the years, God has called me to different assignments. I have served as a home mission pastor, overseas missionary, college professor, and pastor again. Don't lock yourself into a schedule or a setting that God may want to change after a reasonable period. God needs you to be open to His call so He may create in you new adventure, new growth, and new fulfillment.

God requires different things from different people. He places heavier burdens on some, but He never assigns us responsibility without providing adequate grace. Some people, even today, are called to literally give their lives for the sake of the Kingdom. Others are called to care for needs that require less than this. Is one person's role more important than the others? Not in God's eyes. Ours is not to debate the value of the tasks Christ calls us to. Ours is to lovingly obey.

God doesn't require overtime, but our insecurities often call us to it. We try to earn God's favor, prove our worth, or compensate for previous failures with "holy overtime"—even though God has not called us to that. In the Old Testament, Samuel spelled out the principle which counters this human tendency to compensate: "Behold, to obey is better than sacrifice" (1 Samuel 15:22, KJV). If Samuel were speaking to us today, he might paraphrase the principle in this way:

"Listen! Seeking, finding, and obeying God's will in ministry is all it takes. You don't have to work a martyr's schedule."

Johann Sebastian Bach, whose beautiful oratorios have outlived the centuries and are recognized as masterpieces, always wrote at the top of the score, "To the Glory of God." May God help us live our lives of ministry so that we can write the same dedication over the hours and years of our service to Christ.

---

1. Reprinted by permission from *How to Stop Procrastinating and Start Living,* by Loren Broadus, copyright 1983, Augsburg Publishing House, Minneapolis.

2. Reprinted by permission from *Group Magazine,* copyright 1982, Thom Schultz Publications, Inc., Box 481, Loveland, CO 80539.

Chapter 10

How Do You Spank a Church Member?

by Harold Bonner

*Background Scripture: Matthew 18:15-17; 2 Thessa-
lonians 3:6, 14-15*

NOT LONG AFTER Reuben Welch became a college chaplain some of his pastor friends asked what he did in his new
assignment. The gifted preacher cited the classes he taught,
spoke of his role in chapel, then added that he spent a great
amount of time counseling students.

"But what else do you do?" his friends pressed.

He thought a moment, then replied, "I cry a lot."

How do you spank a church member? The same way Reuben Welch counsels—with tears. The answer to this question is
not an easy one to find. And when you do find it, you'll also find
anguish, pain, suffering, and a river of tears.

Given the hard realities of broken vows and spiritual delin-
quency, and given the need to care for the flock with biblical
authority, discipline has to exist. But always it must be in the
spirit of prayer, strong love, and redemption. Discipline pro-
tects the witness and life of the Church. But it also encourages
the offender toward a spirit of repentance and, with that, re-

stores him to his abandoned place in the fellowship of the people of God.

Facing the Problem

It would be wonderful if spiritual backsliding and glaring disobedience to God's Word and God's will never happened. But such an ideal belongs to the world to come—not to this world where even the treasure of salvation is cargoed in "earthen vessels" (2 Corinthians 4:7, KJV). Satan still cunningly pursues his ugly business of deceiving and damning. None are exempted from his attacks. When you consider the many urgent needs of the human spirit, the powerful influences of our secular world, and the twist in human nature, then you clearly see the potential for spiritual failure. But failure is not inevitable. There is a grace in Jesus Christ that is greater than the power of the enemy (1 John 4:4). There is a power through the indwelling Spirit that is able to keep us from falling (Jude 24). Backsliding ought not to be. It does not have to be. But, sadly, it may be. No fellowship of Christians I know of is exempt from having to deal with it.

So, how do you spank a church member? Obviously, we are talking about issues of blatant disobedience and violation of biblical morality. Such categories could include sexual misconduct, business dishonesty, unchristian habits, or the torment of the church by a life of gossip or slander.

Most often these occur at the outer edge of the circle of Christian fellowship. It is out there where people coming to Christ are trying to break the patterns of an old life where He was not, in order to establish the new life where He is. It is out there where the rebellious prodigal is found, marching away from the Savior with his eyes fixed on a far country and his wayward heart caressing a distorted dream. In either case, I doubt that discipline would help. The one coming into new life in Christ needs training, counsel, and direction—not a verbal spanking. The drifting one has usually already dropped out of the fellowship and therefore could care less about rebuke directed toward him from a group he has already forsaken.

But, we must admit, there are those occasions when spiri-

78

tual collapse takes place within the functioning core of the Body of Christ. This happens when someone continues to be active in the church while practicing an unchristian life-style. It is at this point where the matter of discipline comes into its necessary but delicate ministry.

One evangelical church I know of gives the following preface to its policies on church discipline: "The object of church discipline is not the punishment of offenders, but vindication of the truth, purification of the church, warning of the careless, and reformation and salvation of the guilty."[1]

The first example of discipline in the New Testament Church is recorded in Acts 5. Ananias and Sapphira were guilty of deception, what Peter rightly identified as lying to God (v. 4). On that occasion the Church called attention to the sin, but the strong judgment was carried out by God. And the harsh lesson remains: Sin in the Church is no little thing. In some way, it has to be faced and dealt with. Writer C. S. Lewis commented: "A wrong sum can be put right; but only by going back till you find the error and working it afresh from that point, never by simply going on. Evil can be undone, but it cannot 'develop' into good. Time does not heal it."[2]

The Bible on Discipline

Church discipline is not a popular subject. Evangelist Luis Palau calls it "one of the least talked about subjects within the church."[3] Presbyterian Pastor Ben Patterson says flatly, "Church discipline is on the wane in most circles, if not ignored outright."[4]

But the Bible does not ignore it. Let us look at four passages which speak to the issue.

Matthew 18:15-17

"If thy brother shall trespass against thee, go and tell him his fault between thee and him alone: if he shall hear thee, thou hast gained thy brother.

"But if he will not hear thee, then take with thee one or two more, that in the mouth of two or three witnesses every word may be established.

79

"And if he shall neglect to hear them, tell it unto the church: but if he neglect to hear the church, let him be unto thee as an heathen man and a publican" *(KJV)*.

The setting of this passage is one in which the Lord Jesus talks about the sin of one person causing another one, specifically a "little one" (v. 6), to stumble. Such offense, Jesus said, was so terrible that it would be better to hang a millstone around the offender's neck and drown him in the sea (ibid.). Sin is no little matter.

But the stern response Christ calls for is wise and measured to the need. First, He calls for one-on-one discussion of the offense. How often God uses that loving but direct confrontation to lead the offender to a place of repentance and restoration. If you have been wronged, Christ instructs, talk to the wrongdoer—not to others.

Second, Jesus says that if the one-on-one confrontation does not resolve the matter, it should be widened to include one or two others. This, of course, conveys to the person at fault that the wrong is more than just a personal issue—it is a spiritual shadow on the body of the church.

Third, Jesus counsels that if this fails to produce proper Christian change, the matter should be brought to the church. Then, if the person does not submit to the voice of the church, he should be released from the fellowship.

But let us remember that the intention of this kind of confrontation is for the purpose of restoration, if at all possible. Dismissal comes only if all other avenues of healing have failed.

Galatians 6:1-2

"Brothers, if someone is caught in a sin, you who are spiritual should restore him gently. But watch yourself, or you also may be tempted.

"Carry each other's burdens, and in this way you will fulfill the law of Christ."

Here again the clear expression is that sin in the lives of believers is abnormal and should be dealt with for the good of the individual and the community of faith.

Paul places the responsibility for confrontation on spiritual people, that is, those with the maturity to understand, the wisdom to guide, and the indwelling Spirit to provide channels of God's rebuke, concern, and restoration. In the life of the church, this exercise could be carried out by loving, concerned believers who know the offender well enough to have his respect. But in grievous cases, this task could fall to selected members of the church board who share with the pastor in the responsibility of church leadership.

The apostle Paul adds a note of caution that such occasions be marked by the spirit of "meekness" (KJV) or "gentleness" (NASB) on the part of the spiritual ones. These mature Christians should remember that, but for the grace of God, the roles could be reversed. Wrote the Quaker poet John Greenleaf Whittier:

> Revile him not, the temper hath
>   A snare for all;
> And pitying tear, not scorn and wrath,
>   Befit his fall!

1 Corinthians 5:1-2

"It is actually reported that there is sexual immorality among you, and of a kind that does not occur even among pagans: A man has his father's wife.

"And you are proud! Shouldn't you rather have been filled with grief and have put out of your fellowship the man who did this?"

Ancient Corinth had the reputation of licentious immorality. Its temple to Aphrodite had 1,000 priestesses dedicated to prostitution. Corinth was so caught in its frenzy of sexual freedom that among the people of that day "to Corinthianize" meant to "corrupt morally." In that wild city the apostle Paul established a thriving Christian witness. But it was a church scarred by serious problems that needed resolution. One of those problems was the continuing moral decay of many new Christians who failed to see the difference between the new life in Christ—marked by holy living—and the old life of the world—identified by unrestrained indulgence.

The flagrant sin was incest—a man living with his father's wife. Such a relationship was not only forbidden by Old Testament law (Leviticus 18:8; Deuteronomy 22:30), but even the morally corrupt Romans had laws against it. Hence the point of verse 1, that not even pagans do such things. Added to the obscenity of this was the consenting attitude of others who were well aware of the sinful situation. They, Paul said, were not only unashamed, they were actually proud. Both were in need of discipline.

In view of the gravity of the situation, Paul immediately confronted the issue and called for the prompt expulsion of the couple from the fellowship. Sin is too contagious to be treated casually. The pattern has always been that if we allow ourselves to tolerate what we ought to abhor, we may soon come to embrace it for ourselves.

Paul's point is that while we cannot govern the life-style of those who are not Christians (vv. 9-11), we have in the church a responsibility for maintaining the integrity of the Christian witness and for dealing with those who abuse the faith by open and continued ungodliness (v. 13). But if that offender by the grace of God were to repent and turn from his wicked ways, the apostle would have been, without doubt, among the first to welcome him back with open arms (2 Corinthians 2:10).

2 Thessalonians 3:6, 14-15
"Now we command you, brethren, in the name of our Lord Jesus Christ, that ye withdraw yourselves from every brother that walketh disorderly, and not after the tradition which he received of us. . . .

"And if any man obey not our word by this epistle, note that man, and have no company with him, that he may be ashamed.

"Yet count him not as an enemy, but admonish him as a brother" *(KJV)*.

Here again the apostle is urging the ultimate form of discipline—the separating of the offending one from the fellowship of the church. But it is no rash action. It presupposes all that has been advised in Matthew and Galatians. It assumes a knowledge of the truth as set forth in the Epistle and a callous disregard of it.

When there is no turning from wrong, no change of conduct, then the last option is the closed door. But even having said that, the love of Christ bursts forth with a parting note of hope—"count him not as an enemy, but admonish him as a brother."

Such then are the biblical principles of Christian discipline for the church toward the backslider—confrontation and communication:

1. In the spirit of love
2. With the fewest people possible
3. By caring spiritual people
4. In the redemptive reach of Jesus
5. For the purpose of restoration

Only if all of this fails is the decree of separation in order. And even then, the prayer is not for punishment but for protection of others and the eventual return of the prodigal to Christ.

Forming the Fellowship

It is important to understand the biblical principles of "spanking a church member," but it is just as important to remember how we are to nurture the Christian so he will not become entangled in the snares of the world.

Teach Clearly. Twentieth-century people, like first-century ones, need to be taught the Christian faith clearly. The Church, both pastor and laymen, pulpit and classroom, have the charge to "preach the Word; be prepared in season and out of season; correct, rebuke and encourage—with great patience and careful instruction" (2 Timothy 4:2). What we believe and how we should live are the enduring themes of our Christian faith. They should never be silenced.

William McCumber, editor of the *Herald of Holiness,* tells about attending a tent revival that featured the testimony of some local celebrity each night. One evening a well-known athlete testified with these words: "The happiest day of my life was the day I found out that I could go on sinning and still be a Christian." He certainly didn't get this kind of theology from the teaching in his holiness church. Dr. McCumber commented: "Scripture does not permit us to change the court to suit our shots. Over against every compromised life and doctrine stands the unalterable demand of God, 'You shall be holy, for I am holy' (1 Peter 1:16, NASB). Sin calls for repentance, not for redefinition."[5]

Encourage Often. Life can be at times so hard and disappointing. It is precisely at such moments that Satan plays his most enticing tunes. What people need then is the warm, strong word of caring and confidence. Who knows how many Christians have come through crises of the soul because in the midst of their struggle caring brothers gave them smiles instead of slaps.

The Early Church was indebted in no small way to a Christian whose name was Joseph. His constant style of boosting others earned him such a positive reputation that the apostles gave him a new name, Barnabas, "Son of Encouragement" (Acts 4:36).

Love Always. Love is the strongest force in the world. We are taught by the Lord Jesus Christ to demonstrate His life of love as the evidence of our own discipleship (John 13:34-35). Even when we are not sure of precise solutions to delicate matters of human relationship, we can still live in love.

Indeed, if the mending of such broken relationships is ever to occur, it will happen because the Holy Spirit is at work through the healing power of strong, authentic, Christian love. "Love knows no limit to its endurance, no end to its trust, no fading of its hope; it can outlast anything. Love never fails" (1 Corinthians 13:7-8, Phillips).

---

1. *Manual of the Church of the Nazarene* (Kansas City: Nazarene Publishing House, 1980), 219.

2. C. S. Lewis, *The Great Divorce* (New York: MacMillan Publishing Co., 1946), 6.

3. Luis Palau, "Discipline in the Church," *Discipleship Journal* 16 (July 1, 1983): 18.

4. Ben Patterson, "Discipline: The Backbone of the Church," *Leadership,* Winter 1983, 109.

5. William McCumber, "A Bad Solution," *Herald of Holiness,* October 15, 1983, 16.

Chapter 11

Why Have a Revival When the Sinners Won't Come?

by Ralph Neighbour

Background Scripture: Proverbs 16:18-19; Acts 2:42, 46-47; Revelation 2:4-5

OUR FOREFATHERS were much more creative than we are in reaching unbelievers.

Consider the religious climate of their day. Theirs was a God-oriented age, when the occasional atheist in the village stood out like a sore thumb. Almost everyone *believed* in God, whether they were willing to be His true followers or not. The Bible had not yet been attacked by Wellhausen's higher criticism (this did not begin until 1880), and it was readily accepted by most people as the authoritative Word of God.

Moreover, the minister often ranked first in prestige within the community. He was usually an educated man among the uneducated, called on not only to teach and preach, but also to give advice to unschooled members concerning financial and even legal questions. *Elmer Gantry* had not been written, nor had the Protestant church been used for personal profit by entrepreneurs.

Modernism reared its ugly head late in the century, but until the end, the climate for evangelism was one which could presuppose that sinners basically *believed* in heaven, hell, the resurrection of Christ, and His virgin birth. Preaching and methodology reflected this.

Consider also the social climate of that day. There were few outlets for entertainment or diversion. People did not travel far; news was not yet carried with the speed of light. The family was an integral unit, and people usually spent many evenings at home, uninterrupted by PTAs, clubs, political meetings, and so on. "Going out" was an event.

God's men in that culture found a vehicle which was truly God-sent. Called a "revival" in the South, "evangelistic services" in the North, country towns and cities, too, were invaded by weeks of great preaching and singing. A "brush arbor," a tent, or even a wooden tabernacle was erected, usually following the harvesting of the crops.

It was a festival period which often surpassed the circus and the traveling theatrical group in attracting crowds. Methodists, Baptists, Presbyterians, all came; it made no difference what one's denomination was, for these services were the social gathering places for all people in the area. With no radios, gramophones, or other forms of entertainment, these meetings were both social *and* religious. People were content to listen to the marvelous singing of the quartet or soloist, the accomplished playing of a specially imported pianist, and the colorful preaching of a minister who often had developed his own ability as a showman as well as a Bible expositor.

These meetings were often "protracted," a word meaning that they went on for many weeks. One description of them indicated that the minister would preach a solid hour each evening for the first two or three weeks, teaching the Bible principles of salvation and sanctification to the audience. Then, for another week, he would preach 40-minute messages which were directed at backsliding church members.

One report of this period suggests that people would leave each night deeply distressed over their own lack of concern for the lost, their selfish patterns of life, and unconfessed sins.

Invitations following the sermons did not begin in the protracted meeting until people began to *insist* that they were needed, perhaps three weeks after the services had started. By this time, the mind and the emotions had been touched by the messages, and decisions were deep and long-lasting.

Then the minister's messages would be reduced to 20 minutes in length and would usually be a loving, gentle appeal to follow Christ; the invitation could easily consume 45 minutes to an hour. The meeting would then continue for as many days—or weeks—as the "spirit of revival remained" in the town.

In the passing of days, the revival meetings and protracted meetings were less and less effective in reaching sinners. Theater, cinema, radio, phonographs, increased transportation methods, and enlarged educational facilities all contributed to changing the American culture. People no longer met in masses following harvests. The social climate changed. Life became pressured. Skepticism leaked into the college set from professors who openly challenged the very roots of Christendom.

The effectiveness of the meetings waned, and so did their length. People no longer lived such unpressured lives, and the meetings were shortened from six weeks or longer to three weeks, then two weeks, then to the current schedule of one-week meetings. Often nowadays churches schedule weekend emphases.

Large groups of unchurched are never reached by today's revival meeting. They are warned that a revival meeting is coming to the local church on the corner by large signs advertising "REVIVAL!" and portraying mug shots of a preacher and a singer, and they decide to stay away—by the thousands!

Married to the method which was so effective in another age, the church leaders were hesitant to give it up. The creative capacity of our forefathers far and away exceeded anything we have known thus far in evangelism today, and we have not shown the same capacity to innovate in this entire century in a manner equalling that included in our inheritance.

In order to preserve the action of these meetings, all sorts of gimmicks were added: "pack-the-pew plans"; and special services during the Sunday School hours for children aged 8-12, in which pressure was often placed upon youngsters to come forward and be saved. Many came forward and were reported in the magnificent "harvests" of sinners. More and more, the services were attended just by members of the church.

New phrases were born, such as the "inside census" in which lists were made of members' relatives not yet converted and those who attended the church services who were as yet not members. Extensive visitation to these people produced results worth reporting to the other ministers of the area—but no one mentioned that these were, indeed, "church-oriented" people who were being converted by the meetings.

A blind spot had appeared among many ministers. They were not willing to admit they were preaching to the segment of the community still church-oriented. Quietly, large masses of the American population had tiptoed over to the non-church-oriented, skeptical, cynical side; for a long time it seemed the church did not even know what had happened.

Ministers in evangelical churches today are confused about what they should do with the revival meeting. Should it be directed to sinners who are not present, using evangelistic messages which are quite simplistic to an audience usually comprised of the most faithful members of the church? Or should the emphasis be on a "deeper life" message to help Christians grow? Can both emphases possibly be combined in one short week of time? Most people who are truly faithful to the services are not able to attend more than 70 percent of them, due to the competition of secular responsibilities.

Unlike "yesterday," the revival meeting is in trouble with competition nearly every night of the week and every week of the year. PTA, band practice, Little League practice, athletic competition at the local high school, homework, garden clubs, civic clubs, women working days, men out of town for the week on business—the list of reasons may well be endless!

In our world, the family of God has a real struggle to get together on a regular basis to do something as a congregation during the week. For them to be involved in any significant amounts of involvement with unbelievers during the week, in addition to attending the services and singing in the choir, requires superhuman energy.

This writer wants to state vigorously and vehemently that he does *not* feel it is time to do away with the revival meeting. It is almost the only thing done in most evangelical churches in this generation which still concentrates on the reaching of unbelievers. To simply abolish it because it is "outdated and outmoded" would be a colossal disaster! Many church-oriented people can still be reached by these services, and surveys I have taken in scores of churches indicate that the great percentage of their present faithful church members were reached for Christ and made their decision during a revival meeting. This points up the fact that it is just about the *only* thing of worth we have been doing to reach unbelievers. It does *not* reveal the huge vacuum we have left in evangelism by limiting ourselves to revivals as the major method of outreach of the church.

Many areas of our nation still remain where the society is comparatively unhurried and still quite rural in context. In these areas, revivals are far more effective than in the cosmopolitan cities, and they may well be vital in reaching unchurched people for another full generation. City-wide meetings continue to be an excellent cooperative way for the gospel to be communicated to the unchurched, especially when the stadium meeting can be televised live to thousands of homes in the area.

Many ministers have realized that the basic nonreligious reason for unbelievers attending revival meetings has always been for entertainment. They are alert to what can happen by inviting an unusual speaker who has achieved some secular notoriety—like a pro football player, a former movie star, a well-known recording artist, and so on. This awareness has resulted in bringing in large crowds to services. Although such crowds are usually composed of Christians from sister churches, whenever there is motion, some unbelievers are going to be swept into the services and a few converted.

Occasionally in our generation we have been given God-led men who not only have the ability to communicate the gospel effectively, but who have also developed the ability to entertain.

Evangelists who include folk singers in their meetings and who know the problems of today's teenagers reach out to thousands of young people unreachable through routine meetings. Men who are colorful, courageous, and truly sincere in their ministry should be honored guests in the churches of this generation. They have enough sense to realize that men have never enjoyed reading a poorly printed magazine or watching a black and white film when they could see it in full color. They have developed their talents and skills in order to reach men otherwise unreachable.

God bless 'em—and a bushel of onions to those who think they are too flamboyant or too "fleshly."

When meetings are scheduled with the right kind of preparation and the right kind of preachers, they still work. When they are not, they are a real embarrassment in lack of response by both friend and foe.

Having thus protected myself from the barrage of criticism which would otherwise have resulted from this chapter, let me move on to make a very important point: *We are not innovating creative methods of reaching unbelievers in this present generation!* Ours seems to be that in-between age when we are running out of last century's methodology but have not yet become desperate enough in our souls to confess that we are leaving our generation practically untouched with the gospel.

As with alcoholics, so with the church: Until we "bottom out" and are ready to truly admit that we have failed in our task of evangelizing this present generation, we will not become creative or God-directed, as our forefathers were.

New methods of reaching people must be a very real part of the culture of our time. We live in a skeptical, humanistic, technological society. For the first time in the history of America, we must explain why Christianity is superior to Buddhism and Hinduism to many young people who have been converted under our very noses to these Oriental faiths. They do not especially care to hear a soloist sing "The Love of God" and hear a preacher urge them to have sins forgiven; they would much prefer an opportunity to have "eyeball to eyeball" conversations about the entire matter, where penetrating questions can sift through the verbiage of sermons, where truth can be forced to stand simply because it is truth, not just a tear-jerking illustration.

This generation of nonchurched people is the most needy in the history of the human race! They have not found any answers, and they are looking desperately for some way out.

In visiting a crash pad some time ago, I was impressed by the fact that *every room* in the old, dilapidated house which was the scene of action for some 15 or so dropouts from our society included at least one hand-painted picture of Christ on the Cross. Although these young people were violent in their castigations of the church, they obviously were haunted by the Christ. They are a part of the huge group of people today who are not in the slightest way interested in getting dressed up and attending a carefully designed, one-way-communication evangelistic service at a time arbitrarily set by the minister or church council.

I have spent countless hundreds of hours in bars, taverns, private clubs, strip-tease joints, crash pads, and in parks and picnic grounds talking to the unchurched segment of our society regarding their feelings about Christ and His Church. After years of doing this, I am absolutely convinced that the major cause for this generation's being lost to Christ is the fact that *we* are a generation of Christians without the Spirit of Christ upon us, copying an earlier generation which was led by that Spirit, copying the methods that the Spirit gave that generation, and utterly blind to the horrible tragedy we have caused by our own inept and unbroken lives.

Unless and until we "bottom out" and are ready to confess our sin of pride and self-satisfaction, all the new methods and techniques, all the gimmicks and programs will continue to be man-made and not Spirit-given.

Renewal Clues

I shall forever be indebted to the man who introduced me to Eric Hoffer's writings! In the process of reading his *True Believer,* I discovered some pretty obvious things about renewal problems.

In any given structure of society, he says, there are those leaders who have struggled up from the basement of nothingness to the high tower of success. Often this has taken years and years to accomplish. They know every stone in the foundation of that structure and hold sacred every beam and board they walked on as they ascended the stairs to reach their pinnacle. They worked hard to get to "the top."

When someone comes along and suggests that the tower needs a remodeling job, he is immediately viewed as the enemy! What? Touch these sacred and hallowed walls, these foundation stones, these painfully ascended staircases? Certainly not! Does this proposer of the new not recognize the famous names of the past who helped fashion the walls? How dare he suggest renewing them?

Hoffer suggests that those who propose the remodeling are usually those who have not yet climbed out of the basement. They are at the beginning of their ascent to the towers. Since they have not yet invested blood, sweat, and tears in the old structure, they have no sentimental attachment to it. They evaluate it without emotion. It matters little to them whether the building stands or falls. They wish to climb up to their *own* successful position and can be pretty ruthless in doing it.

As a result, those in the basement and those in the tower become enemies of each other. The struggle begins, with upheaval and revolution. Eventually, those in the tower are either deposed or die of natural causes, leaving the tower unoccupied. Those in the basement, previously unsentimental and unattached, move up to the tower—and become viciously defensive of the hallowed walls, foundation stones, and painfully ascended staircases! The cycle occurs again—and again.

Hoffer's insights prove to be so true in church life! A new minister comes to the church and suggests that some changes should be made. The deacons in the tower tell him of how many years the old ways have worked. He soon learns that change is not possible.

The young people return from a thrilling retreat at church camp. Many of them have started to glow with the indwelling presence of Christ. They wish to organize a prayer meeting, a

92

street meeting, a social service ministry. They face the animosity of those in the tower. They are told they are too young; they are too emotional; this will wear off in a few days.

Sure enough, it does!

A layman gets an exciting idea for a new ministry. Seamen on the ships at the wharf arrive daily from across the world. Is there a way the pastor can help him organize and train a group of men to visit sailors on their ships, to distribute Scripture portions in the various languages of the world? Could they not become missionaries without ever leaving town?

He faces the man in the tower.

He is told that *(a)* there is no budget for this; *(b)* these men would never become a part of the local church, and we are not really reaching the people on our own church field; *(c)* such an idea would have to be approved by the church council; *ad infinitum.*

The layman returns to his silent pew.

Renewal will not come in all its fullness to the church until those in the tower leap out to their spiritual death in Christ! When the church has leadership which has been crucified with Christ, it will have no further reputation to protect and no personal interests to shelter. Then the church will begin to move out to love the unloved.

Someone has said there are three things true about a man on a cross: (1) he has no further personal plans; (2) he can look in only one direction; and (3) he is never going back where he came from.

When men in the church become interested in the kingdom of God rather than their own personal kingdoms, the gates of hell are going to feel the impact!

Adapted from *The Seven Last Words of the Church,* by Ralph Neighbour, Chapters 13—14. © Copyright 1973 by Broadman Press. All rights reserved. Used by permission.

Chapter 12

Is Ministry a Nice Word for Manipulation?

by C. S. Cowles

Background Scripture: Romans 15:7; Colossians 2:8-23

ITEM. Prominently displaying the work of vandals who had toppled their gigantic transmission tower, a well-known electronic church evangelist made an emotional appeal for funds on prime-time television. "Will you help me rebuild the tower," he pled, "in order that our worldwide ministry may continue?" Later I learned the tower was fully covered by insurance.

Item. At her own expense a preministerial college student traveled to a distant church to work as a summer ministries intern with children and youth. Instead she spent the summer painting classrooms, mowing lawns, doing custodial work, and baby-sitting in the nursery through the Sunday services. When she gently complained, about midsummer, she was rebuffed by the pastor who questioned the level of her commitment to Christ.

Item. About three weeks after accepting a Sunday School teaching assignment, there arrived in the mail a "Teacher's Covenant" which my friend was asked to sign. Among the three pages of single-spaced rules and responsibilities was a pledge—

not only to attend all the services, but to be available for church work five nights a week and at least a half day on Saturdays. This particular man was already working at two jobs in an effort to support his wife and three children.

Item. Before leading the church in prayer the minister asked everyone to join hands forming an unbroken "chain of love-support." On one side stood my wife whose hand it is always a joy to hold. On one side stood a woman whom I had not yet met, about my age, and presumably married. Now how does a married man go about holding the hand of a married woman not his wife in the closed-eyed intimacy and emotional intensity of prayer? The most uplifting moment of that prayer was when the "Amen" sounded, thus ending our mutual discomfort. It occurred to me, upon reflection, that everybody went along with this "ritual of togetherness," or "caring on command," except the pastor!

Item. "Accountability" seemed like a good idea when the young man first joined the discipleship group. He soon began to discover, however, that his zeal to fulfill group expectations—and thus bring a good report—was matched by a corresponding loss of joy and spontaneity in his private devotions and public service. He also became aware of the fact that he feared the probing question or thinly disguised disapproval of his fellow disciplers more than the wrath of God. What had promised to help him grow spiritually was, in fact, strangling him with oppressive expectations—all the more odious because he had entered into it and accepted it voluntarily.

*   *   *

These random examples illustrate how easily ministry—even though nobly conceived and highly motivated—can slip over the edge into emotional entrapment.

Why?

Because ministry has to do with the heart. It calls us beyond ourselves into the realization of our loftiest spiritual potential. It compels obedience and compliance. In short, ministry impacts us where we are most open, most sensitive, and most vulnerable.

95

Ministry is especially susceptible to manipulation because of its inherent social context. It is carried out through the church, which, as a human institution, brings to bear tremendous group pressure for conformity. The danger is that the individual believer's integrity and freedom is violated in the rush to fulfill some grandiose ministry ideal.

Since ministry is at the very heart of what it means to be a follower of Jesus Christ, how are we to go about fulfilling the Great Commission and the numerous biblical imperatives regarding servanthood without manipulative overkill? There are, I believe, some important scriptural principles that will help us establish ministerial priorities which will set people free to discover and exercise their own gifts of Christian service.

First, people are more important than programs. Jesus said, "For even the Son of Man did not come to be served, but to serve, and to give His life a ransom for many" (Mark 10:45, NASB). This verse, which lies at the very foundation of Christ's call to servanthood (vv. 35-45), cuts across some of our most deep-seated conceptions of what ministry is all about. It is universally assumed that all Christian ministry has as its ultimate objective Jesus and His cause, the kingdom of God. The astonishing claim of this verse, however, is that Jesus' cause is man himself! Man individually—the blind, the lame, the leper, the poor, the rich—and man collectively—"to give His life a ransom for many."

The incredible discovery to be made about ministry is that the call to serve Jesus always points back to man: "Truly I say to you, to the extent that you did it to one of these brothers of Mine, even the least of them, you did it to Me" (Matthew 25:40, NASB). This is the "servanthood circle": to serve Jesus is to minister to man, and to serve man is to serve Jesus.

And where is the kingdom of God? "The kingdom of God is within you" (Luke 17:21). That is, the kingdom which we are called to serve is not in heaven but on earth, not in some grand spiritual dimension but incarnate in our fellowman. Theologian Hans Küng puts the matter sharply: "God wills nothing but . . . man's true greatness . . . man's well-being" (*On Being a Christian*, p. 251).

It is clear from the first page of the Bible to the last that man stands center-stage in terms of God's creative, redemptive, and loving activity. God is always at work on man's behalf: calling, forgiving, healing, reconciling, liberating, resurrecting. This is precisely why Jesus "who, although He existed in the form of God . . . emptied Himself, taking the form of a bond-servant" (Philippians 2:6-7, NASB).

And this is the servanthood ministry to which we are called: "You call me Teacher and Lord; and you are right; for so I am. If I then, the Lord and the Teacher, washed your feet, you also ought to wash one another's feet. For I gave you an example that you also should do as I did to you" (John 13:13-15, NASB).

Any call to ministry, then, which sacrifices the person for the sake of the program, or which tramples people in order to serve people, ought to be called into question. It is wrong to coerce compliance to some grandiose spiritual cause when that cause is really to the detriment of the one who has been manipulated!

Naturally, there are times when cooperative effort is called for and organized structures of ministry are necessary. The call to servanthood does not forbid serving together in unity and with a common purpose. It is important to remember, however, that all humanly devised programs pass away—often right before our eyes. People, however, live forever.

Second, servanthood is more important than systems or programs. Christian ministry tends to be especially susceptible to the "seductivity of systems building." The Great Commission, for instance, suggests strategies of evangelism and calls for salvation-plan formulas. The need for spiritual nurture gives rise to all sorts of discipleship programs, growth groups, and Bible study plans. And this is to be praised.

The problem arises, however, when the system itself becomes associated with some kind of mystical power. Then performance becomes the measure of all things. The believer lives for the system, confident of getting some special merit because of abiding by its dictates. While systems do have value in promoting positive structures and in encouraging disciplined Christian behavior, there are some traps in them about which the apostle Paul warns us in Colossians 2:8-23.

1. Systems—even those that promote spiritual values—tend to rob us of our freedom. "See to it," counsels Paul, "that no one takes you captive through philosophy [logical systems] and empty deception" (Colossians 2:8, NASB). "Captive" in the Greek means "kidnap," "enslave," "exploit."

How does that happen?

Systems call for the surrender of a very important element of our God-given humanity: our intellect. In that they come to us already worked out, they require no prior thought—just blind acceptance. And they discourage, if not forbid, critical examination. Since it all fits together in a tight, logical structure based upon supposedly unassailable assumptions, to question any part of the system would unravel the whole. By their very nature, systems discourage independent judgment and demand total compliance. Hence they make us captive.

The proliferation of cults and the tragedy of Jonestown reminds us of the danger of sacrificing our brains in the service of any system!

2. Systems can be "deceptive," according to Paul. How so? Because they are fashioned "according to the tradition of men, according to the elementary principles of the world, rather than according to Christ" (Colossians 2:8, NASB). For all of their spiritual language and even scriptural references, there is the inevitable human tendency to shift our attention from Christ himself to the Christian life, and from persons to principles. It was this subtle but devastating shift from the Creator to an object within creation (the tree of the knowledge of good and evil) which plunged humanity under the shadow of sin and death.

3. Systems bind us under a new legalism. "If you have died with Christ," continues Paul, "why, as if you were living in the world, do you submit yourself to decrees, such as, 'Do not handle, do not taste, do not touch!'" (Colossians 2:20-21, NASB). All systems finally come down to a catalog of rules and taboos which are not a bit different from the old Mosaic law that was—as systems go—a marvelous creation.

Does this mean that all systems are inherently evil? Not at all! "Let all things be done properly and in an orderly manner" (1 Corinthians 14:40, NASB), says Paul. For God himself is orderly, systematic, and dependable in His nature and activity. It is a question of means and ends. Even as "the Sabbath was made for man, and not man for the Sabbath" (Mark 2:27, NASB), so systems are made for man, and not man for systems.

Third, acceptance is more important than expectance. Since Christian ministry boils down to doing something, it is inevitable that "the doing" will be established according to certain standards which imply certain expectations or results. The situation is ripe, therefore, for the work of ministry to become overlaid with heavy guilt feelings. What is accepted as a challenge to joyous service soon is weighted down with the "almighty ought" and the "everlasting should."

Sometimes these expectations are spelled out, but more often they are subtly implied. Since it is entered into voluntarily, more or less, there is an inevitable process of internalizing, or accepting, those standards.

Given the frailty of human nature, we rarely measure up totally to what is demanded. In the gap between the expectancy level and our performance level rushes feelings of failure, guilt, and condemnation. This is met with greater determination which pushes the expectancy level even higher, thus compounding subsequent failure.

How do we escape this vicious circle which robs us of the joy of ministry?

1. We must accept ourselves as Christ has accepted us, "warts and all." "There is therefore now no condemnation," says Paul, "for those who are in Christ Jesus" (Romans 8:1, NASB). Why? Because God, in His marvelous grace, has accepted us totally in Christ before we have had an opportunity to make one praiseworthy move toward fulfilling any kind of servanthood imperative. And that acceptance is in no way conditional upon our performance level. It remains a gift of God's grace as long as we respond in the obedience of faith (Ephesians 2:8-9).

Naturally, the love of Christ will constrain us to share that love with others through positive structures of ministry. Yet we no longer serve just to win God's approval—or man's—but to express God's love. The tyranny of the "I must" gives way to the liberty of the "I may" and "I will." Guilt gives way to joy as we focus no longer on what we have failed to do but on what, by God's grace, we have managed to accomplish.

2. *We must accept others even as we have been accepted by Christ.* "Wherefore, accept one another," counsels Paul, "just as Christ also accepted us to the glory of God" (Romans 15:7, NASB). We must set people free to become who they are in Christ and find their spiritual calling in a context of accepting affirmation. This means freedom to fail or to spurn our invitation without the threat of our rejection. Jesus did not pursue the rich young ruler after he turned away from His gracious offer of eternal life, even though that decision broke the Master's heart.

Strategies of pressure, coercion, and entrapment in the local church may produce short-term gains. But only servanthood embraced in freedom will endure and flourish over the long run. And it is the long run we are on. To loosely paraphrase the question of Jesus, "For what does it profit a church to gain the whole world and forfeit its soul by violating the integrity of even one human being?" (Mark 8:36).

A commandant at Auschwitz, at the end of July 1941, arbitrarily selected 10 prisoners to be starved to death in reprisal for the escape of one inmate. One of the 10, Franciszek Gajowniczek, began to weep, calling out the names of his wife and two children. A Franciscan friar by the name of Maximilian Kolbe, also a prisoner, heard that cry and volunteered to take Gajowniczek's place. Kolbe survived in a basement cell with the other condemned for nearly two weeks without food or water, comforting his fellow victims until a guard mercifully killed him with an injection.

In October 1982 Father Kolbe was canonized by Pope John Paul II who repeated the words of Jesus, "Greater love has no one than this, that one lay down his life for his friends" (John 15:13, NASB). More importantly, Kolbe will stand as another exemplary model of what ministry is all about: not entrapment but ennoblement, not coercion but support, not pressure but liberation.

Chapter 13

Who's the Minister Around Here, Anyway?

by Findley Edge

*Background Scripture: Romans 12:1-13; Ephesians
4:11-14; James 1:22-27*

YOUNG people often struggle with the question about
whether or not they are "called into the ministry." From one
perspective, this is a completely irrelevant question. If a person
has been called by God to be a Christian, then he has been
called into the ministry.

In the doctrine of the priesthood of all believers and God's
call to ministry we find the key to understanding the plan
which God ordained to accomplish His redemptive purpose in
the world. Namely, He is calling a *people* to be the ministers.
Here is the key. This means that *the primary responsibility for
God's ministry in the world is the responsibility of the laity and
not the clergy.*

The primary responsibility for doing God's work in any
given time and place rests upon the shoulders of the congregation—the people of God—rather than upon the church staff.

This is a revolutionary concept which the majority simply
do not believe and certainly do not practice. Most church mem-

bers feel that they fulfill their "work for God" when they contribute their money to pay the salary of the clergy, who thus are freed from other work and are able to do the work of God. There are, of course, those who have become aware that they have a responsibility in addition to the giving of money. They teach Sunday School, work with youth groups, visit, and minister in other ways. But the basic attitude which persists is that the primary responsibility for doing God's work rests upon the shoulders of the clergy.

A hypothetical illustration will prove my point. If, in a given church, attendance at Sunday School begins to decline, if attendance at worship services falls off, if the number of baptisms or church additions decreases significantly, if money for the budget fails to come in, one or two of the most influential members will quietly contact the presiding bishop about his next appointment for the church. Or in those churches that have a congregational polity, the deacons will get together in a secret meeting. The topic for discussion will be, "Maybe we need to change pastors."

Why do the elders and the deacons feel that the problem focuses in the pastor? Because, they say, "That's *his* job. It's what we called (or hired) him to do. If he can't do it, let's get a man who can." Thus we see the basic attitude of the laity revealed.

I am not trying to defend the ministers. Sometimes churches do need to change pastors. But what I am saying is, here is a tragic misunderstanding concerning the nature of the ministry. What is needed is not so much a change in ministers but a fundamental change in the congregation. Actually, what happens for God in that place is primarily the responsibility of the laity, the people of God who have been called by God to be ministers in that place. If God's work is not being done, then it is because His ministers, the laity, are failing to carry out their ministry.

What we all need to understand at this point is that this is not a devious plan which a group of scheming preachers worked up to try to trap the laity into doing work which preachers don't want to do. Neither is it a malicious program planned in some

103

denominational headquarters to tap a vast untapped source of manpower. This is God's design for the accomplishing of His redemptive mission in the world, and we have missed it! It is God's plan, and we have been trying some other way.

If this is true, obviously it must have a basis in Scripture. In Exodus 19 God was calling a people to be for Him a "kingdom of priests" (v. 6). He was not calling a special group who alone would have this responsibility. The emphasis is upon all the people and their calling to the ministry. In Matthew 21, again the emphasis is upon the "people"—a people who would bring forth fruit. In 1 Peter 2:5, 9, we read, "Ye also, as [living] stones, are built up a spiritual house, an holy priesthood, to offer up spiritual sacrifices, acceptable to God by Jesus Christ. . . . But ye are a chosen generation, a royal priesthood, an holy nation, a peculiar people; that ye should shew forth the praises of him who hath called you out of darkness into his marvellous light" (KJV). (Note the close similarity in these verses and in God's call to the original Israel in Exodus 19:5-6.) Here we find God again calling a people to be His people—a special people.

But why? What is the nature of their uniqueness? What is the purpose of their call? God makes this absolutely clear, to "shew forth the praises of him who hath called you out of darkness into his marvellous light." They are to be a "holy priesthood." For what purpose? "To offer up spiritual sacrifices, acceptable to God by Jesus Christ."

There are several questions that need to be asked with reference to these verses. First, to whom does the personal pronoun "ye" (or you) refer? It says, "Ye . . . a holy priesthood." "Ye are . . . a royal priesthood, an holy nation, a peculiar people."

To answer this we have to ask, "To whom was this little letter addressed?" We find the answer in 1 Peter 1:1. "Peter, an apostle of Jesus Christ, to the strangers scattered throughout Pontus, Galatia, Cappadocia, Asia, and Bithynia" (KJV). It was not written simply to bishops or to the clergy. It was written to the scattered Christians. For example, suppose I were to address a letter to "the scattered Christians in New England," or "the scattered Christians in the South," and I were to say to them, "You have been called to be ministers by God. Fulfill your ministry!" Would such a letter refer only to the preachers or to the church staff? Absolutely not. I would be writing primarily to the laity, the people of God. They are the ministers.

This raises a second question. If the layman is the basic minister, what does the text mean when it says he is to "offer up spiritual sacrifices"? One of the functions of a priest was to serve as a mediator, to seek to bring man and God together. Here we find out that one way in which this function was carried out was by the offering of sacrifices. In the Old Testament one of the functions of a priest was to offer sacrifices to God in behalf of the people. The purposes of these sacrifices were to confess sin, to seek forgiveness, and to bring God and man more closely together. Ultimately the purpose of sacrifices was reconciliation. As members of the people of God, we are called to be priests, and as priests we are to offer "spiritual sacrifices." What does this mean and how do we do it?

A clue to the answer to this question is found in the Book of Hebrews where Jesus is portrayed as the Great High Priest. As the High Priest, Jesus, too, makes sacrifice to God in behalf of the sinful people. He, too, seeks to bring man and God together. Thus the Great High Priest goes into the holy of holies to make His sacrifice to God in behalf of the people—and what is the sacrifice He makes? *He offers himself.* He gives His own life.

What is the "sacrifice" which the Christian, as a priest, is to offer to God in behalf of the sinful world? He is to offer himself, his life in ministry. This is precisely what Paul was talking about when he said in Romans 12:1, "I beseech you therefore, brethren, by the mercies of God, that ye present your bodies a living sacrifice, holy, acceptable unto God . . ."

There is, however, a basic difference in the priesthood of the Old Testament and the priesthood of the New Testament. In the Old Testament the priest offered the sacrifice. In the New Testament the priest *is* the sacrifice. He offers his life to God in behalf of the world which God is seeking to redeem. This is what it means to be a minister . . . to be a Christian . . . to be the people of God. It was God's design and plan from the beginning—and we have missed it! When God calls a person to be a part of His people, He calls him to be a minister. The calls are not separate. They are one and the same.

Still another question needs to be asked. If the laity, the people of God, are the basic ministers, is there no such thing in the New Testament as the clergy? Yes, there is. What, then, is their task? This is a fundamental question both for the clergy and for the laity. Many times the clergy, not understanding clearly their role, have let their ministry be determined by the places where the pressures were the greatest. As a result, they have been very unhappy and have found no fulfillment in the ministry. On the other hand, the laity, through lack of understanding, have placed responsibilities upon the clergy which tended to exploit them and did not permit the fulfillment of their call.

It would be a tremendously releasing experience both for the clergy and the laity if both came to understand the nature of the specific "calling" of the clergy. We find the answer to this question in Ephesians 4:11-12, "And he gave some, apostles; and some, prophets; and some, evangelists; and some, pastors and teachers; for the perfecting of the saints, for the work of the ministry, for the edifying of the body of Christ" (KJV). There are three parallel clauses here that seemingly give the functions of the clergy—to perfect the saints, to do the work of the ministry, and to edify the Body of Christ.

We have here what some New Testament scholars call the heresy of the comma. It must be remembered that in the original Greek manuscripts there were no punctuation marks. The way the King James translators punctuated this verse made a very bad translation. Unfortunately the *Revised Standard Version* is not any better. The best translation, in my judgment, is in the *New English Bible*. The *Good News Bible* is a good translation. If I may be permitted to give a rather free translation, we can see the special task to which the clergy are called. God has called His people, the laity, to be His basic ministers. However, He has called some for special ministry. "He called (appointed) some to be apostles, some to be prophets, some to be evangelists, and some to be pastor-teachers. He called (appointed) these for the purpose of equipping the laity for their ministry, and in this way the Body of Christ is to be built up." God has called the laity to be His basic ministers. He has called some to be "player-coaches" (to use Elton Trueblood's term) to equip the laity for the ministry they are to fulfill. This equipping ministry is of unique importance. One is appointed to this ministry by the Holy Spirit, therefore it must be undertaken with utmost seriousness.

This is a radical departure from the traditional understanding of the roles of the laity and the clergy. The laity had the idea that they were already committed to a "full-time" vocation in the secular world, thus they did not have time—at least much time—to do God's work. Therefore they contributed money to "free" the clergy to have the time needed to fulfill God's ministry. This view is rank heresy. If we follow this pattern, we may continue to do God's work until the Lord comes again and never fulfill God's purpose as it ought to be done.

At the present time many people are seeking new ways to prop up sagging organizations. We reach for new gimmicks, new promotional schemes, new approaches to make the work of the church more effective. Undoubtedly we do need new approaches. But we will never be effective in doing the work of God until His people whom He has called to be His basic ministers come to understand their call and commit themselves with joyful abandon to fulfilling that call. No organizational approach nor promotional scheme can take the place of this basic need. We have been relying upon the wrong people to do the work of the ministry.

Not only have we been relying upon the wrong people, we have been trying to do God's work in the wrong place. What does this mean? We have sought to do the work of God primarily in the church when it must be done primarily in the world.

There are two reasons why the ministry of the laity must be primarily in the world. Each of these reasons reveals a fundamental weakness in the present life and work of the church. First, it is in the world where a ministry for God is desperately needed. In the churches we have numerous meetings. We have regular weekly meetings ... special meetings ... meetings on

Sunday and during the week . . . meetings in the morning and in the evening . . . women's meetings . . . men's meetings. We have large meetings; we have small meetings. And if attendance at some of them begins to decline, we have meetings to find out what's wrong with the attendance at the meetings.

In most of our churches we have no dearth of meetings. What, then, is the weakness in our present approach? We have tried to win the world by holding meetings within our church buildings. There is one tragic flaw in this approach—the world does not attend the meetings. The world knows little and cares less about what takes place in the meetings we are so careful to hold in our church buildings. Thus, in these meetings we are simply talking to each other.

The second reason why the ministry of the laity must be primarily in the world is that the world today insists upon a demonstration of our faith before it will listen to our words. This reveals a second weakness in the life and approach of the present church. We are trying to win the world primarily through the use of words. In classes, in worship services, in special meetings, the church is doing a lot of talking. On the radio and television we talk still more. We bombard the ears of people with words, words, words. However, the church is finding it increasingly difficult to get the world to pay any attention to these words. We cry, "Christ Is the Answer." But the world shrugs its shoulders and ignores us. The politicians and men of business make their decisions as though the church did not exist. Parents are becoming greatly disturbed because the youth are tuning the church out as being irrelevant.

In effect the world is saying to the church, If you people have anything, show it. Don't come quoting Scripture or mouthing words. I want to see a demonstration of what you say.

If what I am saying is true, then much of what we are now doing in our church programs is exactly backwards. By that I mean that the present church program points toward what happens in the church on Sunday as being the climax. The pastor works all week preparing his sermon. The Bible teachers study for their teaching task. A vigorous effort is made in visitation to get as many people as possible to attend on Sunday. What happens in the church on Sunday—this is the climax.

Oh, no! This is not the climax. The climax is what happens in the world during the week. And yet, in our present church program all our effort is pointed toward trying to get as many as we can to come on Sunday. Don't misunderstand. I am not minimizing what happens on Sunday. This is important, but it is not the climax.

Let me illustrate. Here is a church where a thousand people attend services on Sunday. They attend Bible study and enjoy what the teachers have to say, and they listen carefully to what the preacher says in the worship service. It's a good day, they feel. Then Monday comes and they go to their work simply to live their lives as good, decent, respectable people. They come back the following Sunday to repeat the same experience.

Nothing really happens. The world is not touched. On the other hand, consider another church that has only 100 in attendance on Sunday. But these people are aware that God has called them to a ministry. They know that their ministry is in the world during the week. While in church they study, worship, and open their lives to an infilling by the Spirit of God. However, aware that their ministry is in the world during the week, their eyes are focused on the world. What is the ministry that is needed? How can they express this ministry? Where is the particular place where the ministry of each one is to be focused? What special plans need to be made? Because of this, what happens in church on Sunday is exceedingly important, but it is not the climax!

When the worship, study, planning, and equipping are completed, they go out to invade the world for God. In stores, shops, offices, factories, homes, farms, each expresses his ministry. Then the next Sunday they return to church. Some are excited because they have experienced a degree of progress in their ministry.

Others are bloody because they were "clobbered" by the world. Wounds are bound up. Experiences are shared. Confession is made. Encouragement to try again is given, and new strength is sought from each other and from God. They study again, make more plans; worship and infilling is experienced; prayer is offered. And they go out again. The focus of their attention is always on the world. What happens in the world during the week—this is the climax.

Such being the case, we need to change the basis for evaluating the effectiveness of the work of our churches. At present we tend to evaluate the success of the church on the basis of how may attend on Sunday. Rather, we need to ask, "What did those who attended on Sunday do in the world during the week?" This is what really matters. True, it is not easy to evaluate, but this is where the eyes of the church must be focused.

We need to reevaluate the meetings of our churches. Are the meetings being held really equipping the laity for their ministry in the world? Apparently not, but if the present meetings are not really equipping people for their basic ministry, then we need to change what we are doing and start some that will equip them for their ministry.